The future of looking back

Microsoft Research series

At Microsoft Research, we're driven to imagine and to invent. Our desire is to create technology that helps people realize their full potential and to advance the state of the art in computer science. This series shares the insights of Microsoft researchers as they explore the new and the transformative.

The future of looking back

Richard Banks
Microsoft Research Cambridge

1

PUBLISHED BY
Microsoft Press
A Division of Microsoft Corporation
One Microsoft Way
Redmond, Washington 98052-6399

Library of Congress Control Number: 2011938219
ISBN: 978-0-7356-5806-6

Printed and bound in the United States of America.

First Printing

Microsoft Press books are available through booksellers and distributors worldwide. If you need support related to this book, email Microsoft Press Book Support at mspinput@microsoft.com. Please tell us what you think of this book at http://www.microsoft.com/learning/booksurvey.

Series Editor: Devon Musgrave
Editorial production: Waypoint Press
Indexer: Christina Yeager
Cover design and series design concept: John D. Berry
Interior design: Kim Scott

To Ken Cook and Malcolm Banks

Contents at a Glance

Contents

What do you think of this book? We want to hear from you!

Microsoft is interested in hearing your feedback so we can continually improve our
books and learning resources for you. To participate in a brief online survey, please visit:

microsoft.com/learning/booksurvey

Foreword

n this world of rapid—and too often planned—obsolescence, where we seem to automatically equate smaller, bigger, faster, cheaper, higher resolution, and so on, with better, there is a certain value in stepping back from time to time and meditating on what words like "better" or "progress" actually mean to us. Not just as individuals— although that is important—but also as a family, culture, and society. As someone who loves old books but who also works in the world of digital technologies, I find it interesting that not only can I read a first edition of the journals of one of the explorers of Canada, but the experience of doing so is significantly better, and more intimate, than reading the same text on the most fancy new gadget. Not that there aren't times when I welcome having the text on a digital device. Being able to search for a particular passage rather than having to rely on my faulty memory, or possibly an inadequate index, is something that I don't want to give up any more than my first edition. But in terms of the experience, the feel of the paper, the quality of the illustrations, and the visceral sense of connection to what I am reading about, there is no competition to the original book. I love, cherish, and regularly give thanks for the connection to the past that the technology from that earlier time offers me.

And to get closer to the point, I also realize that the nature and intensity of that connection would be even stronger if the book had been written by my ancestor, and even more so, had this copy been theirs. From such an example emerges a range of questions that should, but too seldom does, confront anyone designing or purchasing many of the "new and improved" technologies of today. *The future of looking back*, by Richard Banks, offers one of the most literate, thoughtful, and balanced explorations of such questions that I have encountered.

For example, some of my treasured books are well over 100 years old, yet they still function as well as they ever did. There is no dead battery, fried circuit board, or incompatible media that prevents me from picking up on the exact page from which some predecessor may have left off. Now think of the documents, videos, photos, recordings that you grew up with—not just yours, but those of your parents and their parents before them. Does it not seem ironic that chances are, the older the media, the longer they are likely to survive in a usable form? Sheet music from 200 years ago is as good now as it was when it was written. Can you say the same about your laser discs, 8-track tapes, favorite Atari video games, and CD-ROMs?

What Richard does is explore this space in such a way as to judge it in the court of human values, rather than technological specifications or market penetration. And yet, in so doing, he does not present us with a whining tome nostalgic for the good old days. His approach is both balanced and positive. This is no diatribe bemoaning how technology is destroying our culture. It is far more closely aligned to one of my favorite insights, articulated by the historian of technology, Melvyn Kranzberg:

Technology is neither good nor bad; nor is it neutral.

Essentially, Richard's argument is that the future we get is the one that we design. If we ask the right questions and inform our decisions from a careful consideration of our true values, we can shape our technologies accordingly. Most appropriately, he makes his arguments around that most human of values and needs: weaving a thread of connectivity—emotional, intellectual, and tangible—from our past, through our present, to our future.

Legacy is not just what we inherit from those who came before us but also what we leave to those who follow.

What I take from Richard's book is a value statement that I find as provocative as it is insightful: the nature of legacy may well trump short-term coolness, in terms of long-term value. Furthermore, by asking the right questions at the right time, you may not need to pit one against the other.

Thanks to Richard's book, we are far more likely to ask such questions in such a way. For that, we should thank him—we and those who would inherit the richer legacy that could result.

—Bill Buxton
Principal Researcher, Microsoft

Introduction

The way I see it we've been engaged in this long-term drama since the middle of the 19th century. Technologists provide tools that can improve people's lives. But I want to be clear that I don't think technology by itself improves people's lives, since often I'm criticized for being too pro-technology. Unless there's commensurate ethical and moral improvements to go along with it, it's for naught.

And so there's been, in my view, a social contract. As technologists create disruption, the new stuff we bring in is generally better than the old.

—*Jaron Lanier,* The New York Times, *May 25, 2011*

've spent all of my career thinking about how people and technology meet, and most of it has been focused on designing and building tools. Until fairly recently the use of digital technology had a utilitarian emphasis that involved getting something done, as quickly and efficiently as possible. This wasn't a bad thing because it enabled us to find new ways of working and to achieve a great deal.

Now digital things have permeated other part of our lives, too. Through technology we listen to our favorite music wherever we are, record our world through our cameras, watch our world through digital video, and share all of this—and our thoughts about all of this—with others through the Internet. The design of digital systems has shifted focus from building the best tools and toolbox possible to improving and extending the lives we live every day.

This is a book about the extension of the digital to our most human rites: remembering, reminiscing, reflecting, and honoring. It describes a profound shift in our use of digital technology, and it demands—a bit more strongly than Jaron Lanier does in the quote above—that the new stuff we bring in is much better than the old.

Digital histories

Our daily experience of technology is contradictory. We (or at least geeks like me) are thrilled about and constantly expectant of the new possibilities enabled by our digital things. At the same time, those digital things that we have lived with for only a short period have quietly and subtly become mundane and commonplace. Technology now forms an everyday part of the background of our lives and of the world we live in. It has gone beyond being about novelty to impacting many aspects of what it means simply to be human.

We have lived with technology for so long now that we have to deal with our digital things as part of our personal legacy, for example, and as part of the legacies of our family and friends. In addition to the physical things that are part of a person's estate, we are now being left with an alternative footprint, one that is digital and that provides another record of a life while it is being lived and after it has ended. Technology, long a part of the complexities of life, is now even a part of death. The difference between a digital legacy and a physical legacy is my primary interest here. How is this new form of personal history different from the one we have been used to?

This personal digital footprint will offer us new kinds of content and new kinds of experiences for reflecting on our past and on the pasts of our families and our friends. This footprint may record elements of our lives that we never had evidence of before. It may be vaster than our physical legacies because of the large number of digital things we acquire and store throughout a lifetime and that come without the constraints of physical space. In this book I'm primarily interested in this connection with the past, in the sentimental ways in which we might reflect on a life lived. I don't mean sentimental in a mawkish sense, but merely that when we recall the people, places, and things that were meaningful to us, we can do it in a way that is newly reflective and newly emotive.

The lens of a designer

I've heard people who do jobs similar to mine describe themselves as "interface designers," and some call themselves "user experience designers." I've settled on "interaction designer," although it's a term I'm not entirely happy with. Many kinds of design deal with the interaction between people and things. Suffice it to say that my job is to help make it easy for people to engage with technology by designing the parts that they touch and click to make their computers, in whatever form, do what they want. I've been doing that since I joined Microsoft in 1995.

Inevitably this book should be seen through the lens of what I do for a living. I'm interested not only in the changing relationship we have with the past thanks to digital legacies, but also in how the design of systems plays a role in this. What I have written here is intended both for people who have a general interest in the impact of technology on the way we live, as well as for people interested in how we might design new experiences for reminiscing and reflecting that take advantage of the wealth of digital things we are now producing as a side-effect of our lives.

This book is broken into three parts: Part I, "Stuff and sentimentality," deals with the nature of digital things"; Part II, "A digital life," describes the role of reminiscing in our lives; and Part III, "New sentimental things," looks at future possibilities for digital sentimental objects. Each part is made up of a number of chapters, and at the end of each chapter I've tried to include a number of "design challenges" that ask questions and offer design tasks for creating new systems that allow us to fully explore and make use of digital legacies. You can see these as placeholders for tough problems that need exploring and for systems that need designing to help us leverage our digital footprint in the best possible way.

If you are a designer, consider yourself duly challenged by these end-of-chapter questions and design tasks. If you are not a designer, I hope they give you a sense of the opportunity we have to create digital estates for ourselves that provide real value as we use them to remember our own past and the pasts of our family and friends.

Acknowledgments

Microsoft Research is an amazing place to work, with unprecedented amounts of freedom to focus on issues and technology that matter. Thanks to everyone at the company involved in creating this environment, particularly Ken Wood and Bill Buxton, who are huge design advocates. Thanks to Abi Sellen for providing thought leadership in the domain of digital memory in our team and well beyond, and for creating a design-friendly culture with Richard Harper, whom I also thank for his constant probing, as well as his provocative and obscure use of language. Other collaborators in the SDS team include Sian Lindley and Alex Taylor, who do research that is deep and encourages reflection, as well as Phil Gossett, Tim Regan, and Stuart Taylor for providing not only a technical backbone to our work but an excellence in argument. I've had some great interns in Microsoft Research, and Will Odom, Mark Selby, and Kjen Wilkens, specifically, have created work of the highest quality related to the topic of this book. Will constantly digs up the most insightful anecdotes from the field, while both Mark and Kjen have created artifacts of great subtlety.

Outside of Microsoft Research, my thanks go particularly to Dave Kirk, for partnering with me in many of the themes in this book and helping me to get the ball rolling. Thanks to Microsoft Press for triggering the process of writing this book, and particularly to Devon Musgrave, for first approaching me, suggesting this topic for publication, and continuing to carry the vision for the Microsoft Research series as a whole.

Finally, thanks to my family. To my father and grandfather for their legacy, and to my mother and sister for their sense of history and the discussions over who will inherit the Japanese coffee table. Most importantly, thanks to my wonderful wife Shannon and to little Maddie for their support and love. We make a great team.

PART I

Stuff and sentimentality

NOT LONG AFTER HE DIED I found myself rummaging through a suitcase of photos that belonged to my grandfather. It contained roughly 200 shots that he'd chosen to keep through his lifetime, organized into fading envelopes or photo albums with curling pages. This battered old bag was doing the rounds from family member to family member, and now it was my turn to browse. Laying out the photos on the bed in my spare room, I was struck by how little the person I knew was featured. Here were images of someone else.

My grandfather died in the summer of 2006, at the age of 94. He had retired in 1971, one year after I was born. As a retiree I'd known him as someone focused on his family, home, and interests. As a person who rarely talked about his past and who was not much into reminiscing, he seemed to have an infinite amount of time on his hands to spend with his grandchildren and he lived very much in the moment. He was a modest, suburban man. The suitcase, though, told a different story, of a person I didn't know at all. These old photos told the story of a man who had lived through two World Wars, fighting in one of them, a man who'd trained as a pilot in the Middle East, flown bombers across Germany, and test piloted new aircraft. (Figure I-1 shows one of these photos.) I'd seen paintings on the walls of his home showing some of these planes, but I'd never realized before how what he seemed to consider the central period in his life predated me by thirty years. This was the part of his life he'd chosen to keep a record of, and it was also the part that I felt I knew little about.

Figure I-1 Members of 83 Squadron.

So here was a bag of photos that gave me the opportunity to reflect on my grandfather's life, to gain insight on how he'd lived and what mattered to him. Importantly, it allowed me to learn new things about him even after his death.

Objects play odd tricks on the past. They allow us to time travel, but in a way that is unguided and open to interpretation. They give us insight on a life but not necessarily answers. The suitcase raised as many new questions in me as it answered old ones.

I wonder what the equivalent will be to my grandfather's suitcase full of photos for me. What will my family inherit from me at my death? Today the way we live our lives is quite different from the 1930s or 40s. Now we live a digital and technological life. There are many new ways to record our lives and a multitude of ways in which we can store, see, and share these recordings.

The act of browsing my grandfather's past was an entirely physical one for me. There was no virtual component; there weren't any digital artifacts in sight. No transistors or bits. That isn't true of my life. Now the photos I take are digital and are stored on a hard drive, not in a suitcase.

Looking back on nearly 10 years of digital photography in my own collection, for example, my hard drive tells me I have taken about five thousand photos a year on average. If I extrapolate out to an average lifespan for someone of my gender and situation then we see that at the point when I am likely to die my family will inherit roughly 200,000 photos from me. That will clearly be a different experience for them than the one I had with my grandfather's images.

CHAPTER 1

Getting sentimental

This book asks how our experience of reminiscing will be different in a world where the new and the digital replace the old and the analog. Before we get too deep into the digital, though, it's important to get some sense of the role of objects like my grandfather's suitcase. How are they used for reminiscing, both by their creator and by the people who subsequently inherit them? In this chapter I'm going to spend a little time teasing out some of the more important attributes that make this suitcase and its contents matter to me.

Keeping things safe

One key attribute of the suitcase, of course, is that it exists at all. This isn't something we should take for granted. Objects are fragile, and their survival isn't a given. Sometimes objects like this are deliberately discarded, as part of the process of uncluttering our lives. I don't know how many times my grandfather sorted through the things in his life, how often he and my grandmother had a Spring clean in their home and threw things out. I suspect many times. These photos survived all those decision points and made it to me. That seems important.

Sometimes things are lost through no fault of our own. Maybe they're damaged or destroyed. Perhaps they're lent out and never returned. The fact that there's unpredictability to what survives with and beyond us is part of what makes these items more precious to us.

Keeping things for ourselves

Another attribute of the suitcase is that these photos serve a purpose that is tied to personal memory. Photos are about recording people, places, and events, and it seems clear to me that my grandfather kept this set for understandably selfish reasons. He wanted them for himself, for their power to connect him with other periods of his life, to allow him to remember his own past.

Most people are similarly selfish. We make decisions on a day by day basis for what we want to keep in our lives and what we want to throw out. Often these decisions are driven by pragmatism. Is there enough space in the home for this item? Does it still do the job that it is supposed to? Is it redundant? More often than not, though, things are kept for reasons that are beyond function. Sometimes things are kept because of a sneaking suspicion that they are a connection to our past in some way and that somehow throwing them away will cut the cord that ties us to the place, person, or event that they represent. Often we're not quite sure why we keep these things, to what purpose, but they seem too meaningful to simply discard.

We're hoarders by nature, it seems. We keep boxes of items tucked away in basements or spare rooms that are filled with things that we can't bring ourselves to throw away. Objects that tie our memories to events, people, and places can do so through the tiniest of threads, so it can be hard to decide what to keep or discard. We promote some of these items by putting them on display in our homes, too, on bookshelves, on mantelpieces, on our walls, to act as a constantly visible reminder of our past.

To a great extent these things we keep are an investment for future reminiscing. There is some sense that keeping these kinds of items will serve a purpose in the future. These objects imply a distrust of our own memories, or at least a need to provide support for them.

Keeping things for an audience

While there is a selfish component in keeping sentimental objects, a large motivation for people is also in keeping them for others. Sometimes this can be simply for the purpose of telling stories to friends and family, the objects acting as a kind of conduit for tales. They might help trigger the memory of different chapters in a life story; they might give a sense of a different time or place to the audience.

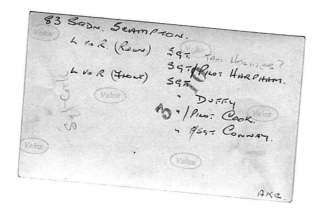

Figure 1-1 The rear of the photograph shown earlier.

I suspect that in addition to keeping them for himself, my grandfather kept his suitcase of photos with some kind of audience or readership in mind. They were organized into envelopes by the different places that he lived. They were very often annotated on the back. While some of this detail was clearly added to support his own memory, some of it seems more unnecessary because he would have known it so intimately. For example, on the back of the photo shown in Figure I-1, he wrote "83 Squadron, Scampton," a detail and location for his crew in the Royal Air Force that he would have known without need of a reminder. (The back of the photo is shown in Figure 1-1.) He seems to have written this with some reader in mind that wasn't him.

I'm lucky that my grandfather took the time to annotate a lot of his photos. The majority of photos don't have this additional rich contextual layer. Instead, we tend to inherit objects whose original use and meaning is lost on us. We have to assume a lot more from what we see.

Although most photos and object go unlabeled, that isn't to say that the desire for this kind of detail isn't there. It's common for people to want to add context and structure to their belongings, even if they often manage to put off the actual activity required to enable it. Photo albums, which many of us create, are often the output when people do actually make time for this activity. They demonstrate a desire to add structure to our images through the laying out of content in an order that makes sense and through the addition of detail to support future storytelling. Photo albums are a desirable artifact to own, since they package up so much detail in one object, but they require effort to make. For every photo album painstakingly assembled, countless more boxes of photos sit unattended, as containers of guilt or hope or wistfulness from which people promise themselves they will "one day" create structure.

While photo albums provide an incredibly rich, almost standalone object for reminiscing, items simply put on display in a home also serve purposes that are directed at others. They might say something to visitors about how the residents of a home perceive themselves or want to be perceived. They invite comment. They offer opportunities for storytelling and conversation.

Objects might be put on display very prominently, where they are easily visible to visitors, or they might be put in the private spaces in a home (in a bedroom, for example). People use space to control their opportunities for storytelling.

Keeping things for legacy

So, objects are kept for personal reminiscence, among other reasons. They are also kept to share with others for the purposes of storytelling. Finally, they are kept as part of a legacy, as an heirloom. But what does it mean to receive an heirloom?

My grandfather's suitcase connected me more closely with my family history, with an individual I knew personally. Yet the fact that this object even came into my hands was something that he never intended and could not predict. I think he had a legacy in mind, but he couldn't have known for certain what shape it would take.

I learned a lot about my grandfather after his suitcase of photos came into my hands. I got some insight into his life as a younger man through the images that I saw only after his death. Through them I could see what periods of his life he cared most about, where he spent his time, what he did, the kind of life he lived. My relationship to him is different now because of what I've seen of him through these photos. Being able to peer into the life he had before I knew him has altered my perception of him. That implies that objects that are inherited continue to play a role in how our relationship with someone develops, even after they are deceased.

In the case of objects that are specifically bequeathed to someone, the story is more complicated because the objects themselves carry a message through the fact that they were left with the recipient in mind. Sometimes the reasons are clear and the recipient knows why something was left for them. Perhaps the bequest is a piece of jewelry that the recipient had admired or an object that represented some shared interest or moment.

Sometimes the reasons for receiving an heirloom are less clear, and this can create a strange state of ambiguity. In the field research that we have done at Microsoft Research Cambridge, UK, for example, we met a person who had been left a box of rocks by his grandfather. Why he'd received this bequest was a mystery to him. If the person had ever had a discussion about rocks with his grandfather, who must have been something of an amateur geologist, this bequest would have made sense, but he hadn't. Neither of them had ever expressed any interest in rocks, but now he has a box full of them and their meaning is ambiguous at best. He keeps them under the bed in his spare room. He can't discard them because he feels some sense of obligation to keep them, perhaps hoping their meaning will become clear one day, but at the moment they are next to valueless to him. He's obliged to keep them, and he's left with the unanswerable question as to why he received them in the first place.

A sense of obligation

This sense of obligation can be quite a common one. Inherited objects often come with baggage, the sense that they have to be kept or put on display because it is expected or is the "right thing to do," rather than simply for personal, sentimental reasons.

For example, a couple we interviewed in our research had adopted a child, and one of the boxes of sentimental artifacts that they showed us didn't contain things that had belonged to the couple but instead was full of toys and clothing that had come with their little boy. These were things that the birth parent had given to the baby. Now they felt they were the custodians of this box of objects and that to some extent they were entrusted with it. They know one day they will give its contents to their child. They have no idea what the response will be or even if their child will feel any connection to what is it contains. Until that day the box lives in their basement and they look after it.

Similarly, we can be driven to put objects on display in our home through a sense of obligation to friends and family. While we might just like to put out the items that are most meaningful to us, the ones that remind us of our favorite events, for example, in reality we often have to display items because we know we should. This is common with photos of family members, for example. It's hard to just put out the best photos of a few family members without feeling some obligation to make sure that everyone in the family is also represented. We imagine the embarrassment of having a family member visit and notice that they aren't represented among a set of photos, while many other relatives are.

Sentiment, not archaeology

My mother keeps a set of family photos on the wall of her dining room that go back a hundred years. I recognize some of the people in them; my grandfather is among them, for example. One older group of photos, though, contains a number of people whose faces I don't know. One shot shows a man on horseback, dressed immaculately in English hunting clothes. Another is a group shot of two women and two men, the two women sitting stiffly on a garden bench, the men standing immediately behind.

I look at these photos and suspect that my mother sees them in a way that is quite different from how I seem them. The man on horseback is her great uncle, for example, a man she knew when he was alive. In these photos she sees people that she knew, even as a small child. I see strangers.

When my mother sees these people she is reminded of how they were when they lived. She can recall how they moved, the sound of their voices, the events that connected her with them, the places she visited that they called home. I don't have these memories of them. My interest in the photos is not in my reminiscences, because I don't have any. Instead, my interests end up being about the details of the photos, the things they tell me about the time in which they were taken. The formality of the subject's poses, for example, which seems so different from the way we might pose for photos today. The way they're dressed, which seems so formal and uncomfortable. Even the quality of the photos, which are faded sepia. My interest in these shots is not in them as objects of reminiscence so much as objects of archaeology.

Figure 1-2 My grandfather's Oxo tin.

This shift from the sentimental to the archaeological seems true of any kind of object, not just items like photos that record lives. My grandfather kept some mundane physical items with his photos that obviously must have had some sentimental meaning for him. For example, one of the objects he kept is a small tin box that used to contain Oxo cubes, used for making gravy. (See Figure 1-2.) It's possible that my grandfather associated this with the period of food rationing during and after the Second World War. Or maybe it was something given to pilots. Maybe he remembered something more specific, like the actual moment of being given it by some friend or relative. The reason he kept it (its story, if you like) is lost now, however. Without that insight this object is merely something that gives me an idea of how, for example, things were packaged sixty years ago.

As objects age they eventually leave the possession of people who can remember them in use or who knew their original owner. Instead, as they change hands they are newly interpreted in a way that is more objective, as the generation that inherits them shifts from knowing their stories or subjects to knowing simple facts about them.

Even if we knew the original owner of an heirloom, or the original subject of a photo, and these items still have sentimental value, an archaeological aspect can start to creep in. I can't look at the older photos of my grandfather without being fascinated by what he was wearing, how he was standing, and so on. This is a fascination not based on the fact that what he wore or the way he was standing reminded me of him, but because that was what people wore or how people stood back then.

In our field research one of our interviewees had inherited thirty or forty years of diaries from her aunt. While there is a lot of deeply personal content in this stack of hand-written books, much of what seems interesting about them to their new owner is in the entries that are more mundane, that describe a day to day routine and a way of living quite different from how we live today. There is an archaeological aspect to this, as well as a personal one. Maybe this aspect creeps in the more the life represented through an object is in contrast to our own. Maybe it requires time to simply pass.

Unexpectedly sentimental

Photos have an implicit value as a sentimental artifact: they capture a place, an event, or a person, and it's understood that at the very least the photographer was there and would be able to reminisce about that moment. (Let us forget for the moment composite photographs artists make, in which nonexistent places are created.) However, it's often quite difficult to know why nonphotographic objects are meaningful to someone, because the most unexpected and seemingly valueless items can be important for reminiscing.

In our field research we asked a participant to show us the most sentimental object he possessed. He unpacked a box of items he'd kept in his basement and pulled out an old, battered and charred plastic gear. It had been part of the first motorbike the participant had owned, which at some point had blown up. He'd picked up this gear from the side of the road where the bike had broken down and ever since had somehow held it responsible for the accident. It became the artifact through which he remembered that period of his life and the event. To another person this item is worthless, but one person's trash can be another person's key to memory. Sentiment, it seems, can be attached to anything.

I talked earlier about how objects shift from a focus on sentiment to a focus on archaeology as they change hands and the memory of them in their original context diminishes. I'm not sure what the archaeological value is in this charred plastic gear. All that matters about it, really, is the story that's tied to it. Once the story dies, so, to some extent, does the value of the item.

Family heirlooms

It's possible that the owner of that gnarled plastic gear has told the story of the event to his family again and again and that the object will continue to matter to another generation because its history has become entrenched and the family understands what it represents. This process of storytelling and inheritance could, theoretically, go on through for generations with each successive owner retelling the story of it again and again.

The class of objects that work this way become family heirlooms because the process of inheritance and storytelling is repeated so many times that family members simply know the story of the object and aren't really sure when they were first told it. These kind of objects have "always been" in the family, and everyone seems to know the stories behind them.

Sometimes the stories themselves are actually lost but the family member simply knows that the object mattered somehow to their ancestors. Knowing that some distant relative owned and used it gives it meaning. It's common for jewelry to be in this state, with engagement rings, for example, becoming part of a family tradition.

There is a question of how our relationship to material things might change the concept of a family heirloom in the future. Will family heirlooms emerge from the new objects we purchase today? Furniture is a common form of family heirloom, with chairs and tables handed down through the generations. Now, though, we tend to refresh our homes on a more regular basis, and furniture tends to be cheaper, arriving flat-packed and ready for self-assembly at home. I can't imagine my Ikea Billy bookcases being something my daughter would want to treasure since in my experience (and I've had quite a few of them) they are not the most robust of items.

Our lives are now full of disposable material things in a way that they perhaps weren't in the past. Will this mean that there are less really precious things that we own and that those few things will become even more special, or will everything we leave behind simply feel cheap?

A sentimental point of view

People of my generation are now at an age where they are starting to have to deal with their parent's mortality. For parents this can involve trying to think rationally about the content of their home, and their estate as a whole, in order to decide what will happen to it all. This can involve uncomfortable conversations in which the parents guide their children around their home and ask them "what they'd like" once they pass away, like some sort of estate sale preview.

Parents in this situation are often surprised to find that the things that they imagined their children would wish to inherit aren't the same things their children actually want. The objects that people want to bequeath to others aren't always the ones that others want to receive. Similarly, parents can have a strong memory of some event in their child's life that their child can't even recall, and vice versa.

Reminiscing and sentiment comes from a very personal perspective, and it's hard to predict.

Heirlooms with function

My grandfather's suitcase of photos is a lovely artifact, but function-ally it is now all about reminiscing. It doesn't serve any other purpose than looking at the past. Many heirlooms, though, continue to serve a practical function day to day even as they act as objects that trigger memory.

One of the people we talked to in our fieldwork, for example, had inherited a ladle from her great aunt. It serves dual function both as a practical object for stirring and serving soups and stews, and also as a connection to the past. She keeps it above her stove and uses it on a daily basis. While using the item, she is reminded of (and can imagine from memories she has as a young child) her relative in her own kitchen using it.

There's something delightful in the fact that these objects can have both practical and sentimental aspects. This can be seen often with tools and implements. Somehow space isn't wasted on them because they are useful and emotive at the same time.

Adding your own layer of sentiment

When objects change hands as part of an inheritance, they enter a new environment and a new life. They don't stop being physical and able to be acted upon. The ladle, just described above, isn't suddenly impervious. Instead, it will probably pick up a few new nicks and scratches as it continues to be used. To some extent these form a new history from a new generation, layered on top of the object's existing form. Similarly, a photo album inherited from an ancestor will pick up scuffs and tears as it is kept on a bookshelf and pulled down for viewing.

For some objects this layering of a new history through use can be a more active process. We talked to one person in our fieldwork who had inherited a cookbook from her mother. It had originally belonged to, and been created by, her grandmother. Each successive generation had added notes to the book, embellishing or even correcting recipes.

This idea that an heirloom can be added to by each generation is a lovely one. It could potentially be a destructive activity, like the worst kind of graffiti. But if it is done sensitively, an object can emerge that is more resonant because of this cross-generational collaboration, representing a shared history rather than the history of one individual.

Hopefully I've given you a sense of how I think my grandfather's suitcase of photos works as an object of sentiment and reminiscing, as well as some insight into what we've learned about the role of similar objects in people's lives.

Heirlooms are fragile and are about the self as well as others. They change nature both through time and through the perspective of the viewer. They need context to survive in a sentimental sense, and they can continue to add to our lives in rich ways as objects of function and objects onto which we can write our own stories.

These qualities and functions seem true of physical things, which we might consider the traditional artifacts of inheritance. Can they be true of digital things, too?

Design challenges

I mentioned in the Introduction that I'd be describing some design challenges at the end of each chapter. Here is the first set. You can think of these as areas for exploration and further thinking, as well as opportunities for new kinds of experiences that help engage people with their past.

→ How might we design new experiences that are focused on personal reminiscing?

→ How might we design systems that allow us to record why certain things are sentimental to us?

→ How might we design digital containers to keep things safe for the future?

Some of the challenges in this chapter deal with the social nature of our heirlooms.

→ How might we design ways to share and tell stories with and through digital things?

→ How might we design ways for digital things to be passed on to others?

→ How might we design systems that remind us of, or help us fulfill our obligations to, others?

→ How might we design ways for families to celebrate important objects together, even if they live apart?

→ How might we design ways that allow parents and their children to express their desires for objects and to partition an estate together?

→ How might we design systems that allow for the layering of stories from multiple generations on an object?

CHAPTER 2

Attributes of the physical and the digital

There is no question that we can feel a deep sense of sentiment towards digital things. In our field research, in which we've asked people to talk about items in their homes that matter to them, they've shown us digital things as well as physical. They've told us about documents written in Microsoft Word that are precious because the words they contain matter; they've described threads of email that record a deeply personal exchange. While the experience of the artifact is different between physical and digital, in the end the content still matters.

People feel the same sense of anxiety about the potential loss of their digital photos through fire or theft as they might with the physical equivalent. Strategies for solving this problem with digital items seem troublesome and burdensome because so many options for copying and backing up exist and most require regular routine while still seeming insecure. Backing up digital photos to a CD, for example, is a process that requires effort and the CDs themselves still feel fragile.

It's worth exploring similarities and differences in our experiences of sentimental physical and digital items. How do the attributes of a digital object change the way in which it might be used for reminiscing or change the way in which thinking about the past might happen more generally?

Let's begin by comparing some of the attributes of physical items to those of the digital to draw out some of the ways in which we might feel differently about them. I'll start with a list of positive attributes of physical things, each of which is (to some extent) a negative attribute of digital things, and vice versa.

What's good about the physical?

Setting aside the vagaries of quantum computing for now, in which one quantum can be in two places at the same time, objects made of atoms are basically unique. **There can be only one of each object.** We may be in an age of extreme mass manufacturing, but when we buy something that's physical there is only one unique version of the item we receive. This can make physical things feel more precious not only because we can hold them but also since there's fragility associated with the chance that we might lose or damage them.

Digital things, by contrast, can be duplicated infinitely, with a simple Copy and Paste. They're made of bits. This has a lot of positive sides to it, which I'll get to a little further on, but from the point of view of sentimentality, their ease of duplication can make them feel cheap.

Think of the difference between owning a vinyl record (assuming you ever have), in which audio is made material, versus owning the audio in a purely digital form in which it has been downloaded to a device and never manifested itself physically. I'm not arguing that the audio itself is any more or less delightful in physical or digital form, but merely that the physical embodiment of audio through an object like a vinyl record can add a new layer of memory to the experience. I remember the ritual of using this kind of object, the sound of putting the needle down on the record to start it playing, small scratches that made a pop at certain points in the track and so on. I still can't listen to certain songs without hearing those pops in my mind. These physical attributes embellished the experience of listening to the music.

Physical things, therefore, **can play on all the senses** through their material attributes. They have a form that can be seen and touched. They can be heard and even smelled. All of these properties can become part of our memory, like the scratches and nicks in the record.

Digital things, by contrast, are experienced to a great extent through the visual sense, primarily through the screen. Digital audio is clear and uncluttered by the physical. Our experience of touching digital things is filtered through an interface, which adds a level of indirection with the object.

In the design of digital things we seem to be constantly searching for something like a physical manifestation to heighten our experience of them. It could be argued that the goal of new touch-based experiences provided through devices like the Microsoft Surface (shown in Figure 2-1) or touch-based phones, for example, is primarily to provide metaphors of physicality that make our experience of content feel more rich and dynamic. Through them we create interfaces that fake gravity, giving digital items a mass and inertia. We can turn them, flick them, and play with them as if they were real objects at the end of our fingertips.

Figure 2-1 Microsoft Surface.

Physical things **take up real space**, and really special things become part of the landscape of our home as they are put on display and celebrated. From a reminiscing perspective this means that we remember meaning not only by reviewing an item's content (for example, in a photo album) but also by recalling spaces the thing used to occupy. An object we've inherited from a family member can evoke memories of the room it used to be kept in at their home. Memories reside in the content and material of an object and also in its connection to various physical places.

I'm not sure we have the same sense of where digital things live. A folder system on a personal computer is a strange place to visit. Like the tip of an iceberg, only a small part of it is visible at any time, the rest hidden away from us under the virtual surface. It's hard to get a sense of how big this body of items is, and it's a tough place to build a mental model of because there are few landmarks to help trigger our sense of place. Each folder looks much like any other.

The fact that physical things occupy real volume means that we are limited in the number we can have. Our homes are only so large, and even with lofts and basements overflowing with stuff we are forced eventually to make decisions about what to keep and what to discard. This is a good and bad thing. Good in the sense that it forces us to filter our content to those items that really matter so that, theoretically, we are surrounded by more meaningful things. Bad in the sense that we can end up ridding ourselves of things that, in retrospect, we would rather we had kept.

We're not driven to discard digital things in the same way. The size of storage media seems to outpace the amount of space we need for our digital things; we can keep pretty much everything for as long as we want. And because one virtual item looks pretty much that same as any other, meaningful digital artifacts can easily get lost since they live alongside the less meaningful. We have to do work to make them stand out, by putting them in special folders or naming them in a way that makes them more unique.

Physical things also **change with time**. Unavoidably, the materials that they are made up of oxidize, creep, harden or soften, fade or crumble away. This can give them an aesthetic of age that makes them somehow more sentimental. It's a visible, material reminder that these are objects of the past, which connect us with people, places, and events we care about.

Digital things, by contrast, are fixed. They are aged by what changes around them. That is to say that they can look outdated, as physical things can, because of how the systems they were part of are replaced or renewed. But the bits themselves do not change their fundamental form. Look back at some of the earliest digital photos, which are black and white, and pixelated. They haven't changed their structure. The bits are still in the same order. But advances in technology make them look archaic.

Physical objects have this aspect, too: **our perception of them shifts as things around them change**. This can be tied in the short term with changes in fashion or with shifts in technology. It can happen for many reasons, and this is a challenge to the survival of an item. Often, the first stage in the aging of an object is simply for it to look out of date and unfashionable. Our instinct at this point is to replace it with something that seems more modern and fresh. Yet with time many of these objects can become meaningful again, as totems that connect us with a particular point in our history or simply as items that suddenly look compelling because of their age. Many of us have items that we wished we hadn't discarded because of how fondly we remember them now.

I collect old transistor 8 radios from the 1950s and 60s. I'm not quite sure why I collect them. Not for sentimental reasons, since I wasn't alive in those decades. But I think they're beautiful. I don't keep batteries in them, since there's the risk of acid leaking out and causing damage to them. So they're serve no functional purpose; they sit on my office shelf as aesthetic objects.

At some point these radios would have been the pinnacle of technology. They were the Walkman and iPod of their day, allowing people to slip an earpiece into an ear and listen (in mono, of course) to the transmission from their local station. At the time that they were contemporary they were in their own technology race, much as cell phones are now, with changes in transistor technology leading to newer and newer models. Maybe they're useful for drawing parallels in how our own modern objects will be admired in the future.

I suspect that the experience of having one of these radios was much like what many of us experience today through our phones. We buy the latest model. It's exciting and new. At some point it starts to look a little out of date, particularly once it's superseded by something newer and shinier. And eventually we discard it because it's embarrassingly old fashioned.

The radios in my collection, some of which are shown in Figure 2-2, seem to have made it through to the other side of this process. They look old, but that's now part of their charm. Their aesthetic appeal is now tied up in the way they represent a certain age and style, as if they'd come off the set of Mad Men. And if I'd actually used one of these radios as a little boy, they'd also act on another level, as a trigger for reminiscing.

Figure 2-2 My transistor radio collection.

In addition to objects aging through changes in the environment around them, they also **acquire a patina throughout their lives.**

Their surface is changed by the way in which we handle them and use them over time. They get shiny at the spots where we regularly touch them, for example. They also get nicks and scratches through accidents and incidents. While on the one hand this surface change can make an object look tired, it can also add to its history and character, reminding us of the stories associated with it.

Sometimes these surface changes are created deliberately, as a form of personalization, rather than by accident. Many old, antique wooden school desks contain in their surfaces the scratch marks of generations of students. I'm not condoning vandalism, but these strata of history tell a powerful story. Being a part of that tale through the scratching in of one's own name is appealing.

Objects can acquire a patina through the removal of material (those nicks and scratches) or through the addition of material, adding new layers onto old. This, too, can be seen as a form of additive person-alization. I have a set of my mother's original Beatles albums. In one corner she had written her surname (her maiden name at the time) in uppercase in ink. From a collector's point of view this probably detracts from their value, but to me it gives a sense of her as a teenage fan. She wanted people to know that these albums were hers. Writing her name on them was a form of personalization that made this set of albums, rather than the millions of others, uniquely her property, and now uniquely mine.

We do this all the time to our objects, of course, as a way of making our objects expressive and uniquely ours. We add stickers to items, for example. And once these objects age, that story of ownership is car-ried with them. It's a form of authorship, putting our own stamp onto something. I'm not sure what the equivalent is in the digital world. My mother's maiden name, in the digital world, is simply a piece of meta-data like any other. If she'd had digital versions of these albums, rather than the physical, perhaps the equivalent would have been creating a folder or playlist in her name and putting the songs in there.

This list of attributes (boldfaced above) of the physical is by no means exhaustive, but I'll stop here for brevity. When it comes to sentimentality, to some extent it feels like the positive attributes are about the fragility that comes through uniqueness and about the malleability of the material. Physical objects change and we change them, and as we do this they can become more meaningful.

I'm not sure the same can be said of the digital. In the next section is a list of some of the positive attributes of digital things, and in looking at them it feels to me that the value that bits bring to sentimentality are a durability in virtual artifacts and therefore potentially in the memories that are associated with them, the possibility for new ways to be sentimental because of new forms of interaction, and the sheer ocean of reminiscing that we may have to swim in because of the scale of our digital lives.

What's good about the digital?

I've described above how physical things age and how that can add to the sense of sentimentality both for the artifact and for the memories associated with it. Digital things are not like that. While digital things are fragile, in the sense that they need to be backed up and looked after to persist, the bits themselves, the things that digital artifacts are made from, are **very persistent**. Digital things stay put, in the form in which they were created, without a creeping in of age that comes about from the material itself, as is the case with the physical.

This can be considered a negative, which is the way I portrayed it earlier, in that the material properties of the artifact don't get richer with time, but it can also be a boon because it provides predictability in reminiscing. We know that what we see now is what will be seen in the future and indeed is what was seen in the past. There's significant reassurance in the fixity of digital things.

But while the material of digital things is persistent, we do worry about the potential loss of the items themselves all the time. So I don't mean to imply that digital things aren't fragile. Cathy Marshall, who has worked extensively in Microsoft Research looking at issues around personal archiving, expresses this risk when she says, "It is these

everyday digital artifacts—the things that people cherish the most—
that would seem to have the most uncertain fate if we simply continue
to move forward on the current technological trajectory." In her work
she describes a broad number of reasons why it is difficult to look after
our digital things. Some of these reasons relate to human nature, such
as our amazing capacity for lack of action in looking after our possessions, which may never change. And some reasons why digital things
feel fragile are technological. But it is possible that our engagement
with the Internet, which continues to accelerate, may provide us with a
new enough technological trajectory that some of the issues of personal
archiving might solve themselves.

One technological issue with personal archiving practices is with the
hardware on which we keep things. We archive our digital items onto
floppy disks, Zip disks, and external hard drives, which become inacces-
sible when the interfaces that they need become outdated. I think it's
likely that this issue will diminish as our perception of storage shifts from
content that is locked away on one machine in a specific location (like
a PC in a home) to it being more distributed (in the cloud). I store a lot
of photos on the Internet, on my website, and on sites like the photo-
sharing service Flickr. I have no idea what kind of hardware my files
are now stored on or even where they are geographically. I just expect
to have access to them as long as I pay my bills. The idea of storage is
becoming more abstracted as we have to attend to it less.

Issues around old versions of files, in which we are unable to open
items we've authored in the past because the tools of today no longer
recognize them, will also diminish. I have files authored in Macromedia
Director and Adobe PageMaker, for example, which I am no longer
able to open. Software is persistent, but it's also **highly malleable**,
and I suspect that as the Internet continues to play a bigger part in our
lives, many of these issues and concerns of its persistence will simply
disappear because of the way we can nearly always change the form
of a digital item if we need to. If an old file in an out-of-date format is
accessible online, in many cases all we need is some software to update
it to the latest accessible version. In the same way that modern software
is often updated or patched on a regular basis with little input from us,

we might even get used to services that continually keep our files up to date for us.

An alternative is to run virtual versions of the old applications and environments that we used to use so that we can get access to our files in their original context when we need to. The great thing about old PC environments is that they have low power requirements compared to modern computing systems. The PC I did much of my work on more than a decade ago had an old Intel 386 processor running in it. Today's PCs are an order of magnitude more powerful, with multiple processors that run much more rapidly. This means that emulating old machines isn't that burdensome. It would be perfectly possible to run my old PC, with all its files and applications, in a window on my new PC, so that I could visit the old environment in which I used to work when I felt like it. In addition to the practical side of this, there's a sentimental side, too. I would have an old "place" where I used to spend a lot of time available to me, and it would enable reminiscing like any other place I might return to.

My first computer was a Sinclair Spectrum with 48k of memory. It was a common entry-level computer in the UK in the 1980s, used primarily for running primitive games. Although it was (relatively) powerful in its day, its operating system is just a few lines of programming compared to modern machines. The memory for the whole operating system of the Spectrum is smaller than the size of most webpages. It's so small that a version of it (an emulator) has even been written in Adobe Flash. If I want to experience the old games I used to play on it in my teens, all I have to do now is visit the right webpage and it is available in seconds.

Making duplicates of digital things is trivial. With a simple Copy and Paste suddenly I can have an object live in two places at once. I can keep one copy on my PC while I put a second copy away somewhere safe. This has always been great for providing some peace of mind in anticipation of the loss of one or other copy, but a second big benefit of this ability is that it makes items **very easy to share**. From a sentimentality point of view, the difficult decisions with physical things about which family member will inherit which item are eased somewhat with the digital because anything sentimental can be duplicated and shared.

Items can be shared more privately, among family members, or they can be shared much more publicly, of course. An item of inheritance like a piece of furniture has to go to one family member, live in one place, and have people visit it to experience it, but a digital item (such as a recording of the deceased) can be sent to every family member through email or simply posted on the Internet somewhere for everyone to experience. This content could be shared openly with the public or access to it could be restricted, depending on the wishes of the family.

Digital things can **have properties and behaviors that bring them alive** on screen. They can react to my touch so that I can drag them around and place them where I want them. They can move themselves if necessary, creating arrangements such as rows and columns that help me when I'm seeking them out. They are unencumbered by the laws of gravity or rules of inertia or force. The experiences we have of them can be dynamic and compelling in a way that isn't possible with the physical.

Think of a simple slide show of digital photos, created to tell a story of an important event. Images can move in and out of view as we advance and retreat through them. They can fade subtly from one to another or be moved or resized to draw attention to some area within. They can have music or voices playing over them; they can include video. Even the simplest of shows is dynamic in a way that isn't possible with physical items. They can play on our senses and provide a layering of reminiscing that is quite different, and potentially more engaging, than, say, a photo album.

While we can create experiences like slide shows that pull items together to tell a story, individual digital items can also **have their properties embedded in them** as metadata. A digital photo can have a title and description and the date it was taken all embedded within it. While an analogue image can have these things written on the back side, like my grandfather's photo I showed earlier, the metadata a digital item can carry is not limited by the item's physical dimensions and can go beyond what we would be able to record through analogue means. Additional details like the GPS coordinate of the location where a photo was taken and the camera model that was used to take it add more and more layers of meaning to the image. Digital things have the capacity to carry these properties with them at all times, even if it requires a bit of effort on the part of their owners to actually sit down and enter these details.

While a slide show, digital or analogue, is editorialized and assembled to create a specific experience—specific items in a specific order— **digital things can also be acted upon in concert**, as live items, which dynamically changes the way we consume them. Before I started storing all my music as MP3 files on my computer, I used to play them on LPs and then CDs. Each set of songs was constrained to the physical storage medium on which it was stored. Now, with all my songs kept in a digital form and in the same place, I can have experiences across my collection. I can automatically play all the songs I own by a particular artist, for example, or all of the albums released in a particular year. Interacting with a complete collection of physical objects is much more difficult and sometimes even impossible.

Our collections of digital things are outgrowing our collections of their physical equivalents. We take and store far more digital photos than we did analogue photos because they are easy to take, free to "develop," and can be stored with little burden. For similar reasons we send and receive far more emails than we ever did letters. Digital objects operate on a different scale in terms of numbers of items compared to the physical, with the result that the way we experience them for reminiscing is quite different. Going through all those items deliberately and individually sounds quite burdensome, but the **opportunity for experiencing them serendipitously** is a compelling one that allows us to dip into our past in a new way. Putting all of my digital photos on random creates a haphazard experience of the things I have done, places I have been, and people I have known. This experience is out of my control, which means that accidental instances of remembrance are created for me that I would have missed out on if all I ever experienced was content that I had authored or accessed deliberately. Likewise, hearing unexpected songs unexpectedly triggers memories of particular times in my life.

Why even limit ourselves to items that are stored in the same location? With the ubiquity of networks, digital things **can be strung together**, connected to many other things that may live nearby or continents away. We can view stories of someone's life that are linear or that branch many times. This could be a story that I created or one that was created collaboratively, with many others adding their own anecdotes and reminiscences. This is a form of sharing and of reminiscence that can be a richer one than simply having a group of people huddle around a photo album sharing stories.

The positive attributes for reminiscing that I described for physical things were mostly focused on the effect that material properties have on our feelings of sentimentality. Digital things offer us more opportunity for the creation of new experiences of our past, experiences that are rich because of increased detail and new relationships created between elements, both of which increase the capacity of a set of digital items to carry a story.

The question is, who is creating these new experiences? One attribute that both the physical and digital share is that they are both commonly objects of guilt when it comes to our plans for how we might use them for reminiscing. Many of us have boxes of old photos in our homes that we plan on creating photo albums from "one day." They sit as constant reminders, yet we never find the time, a symptom of our busy lives. A folder of digital photos that we might want to link in a rich slide show has the same capacity to sit for years, with our best-laid plans never coming to fruition.

The Catch-22 here might be that randomly created, serendipitous experiences fail to give us the time we may need for real reflection with our content. The slow, deliberate creation of an artifact like a photo album gives us time to look at items and piece together in our heads relationships through time and place that we might not otherwise have seen. Physical objects can give us time to reflect, while digital technology can give us new and unexpected experiences. Are there ways of combining both to make our experience of the past a richer one?

Design challenges

The design challenges for this chapter explore the exchange of properties between the physical and digital in order to generate new experiences.

→ Think about the positive attributes of *physical* things discussed above. What might it mean to apply some of these to digital things? What would it mean to design a digital file that is unique, for example, or that ages over time?

→ Think about the positive attributes of *digital* things discussed above. What might it mean to apply some of these to physical things? What would it mean to design physical things that can be connected to one another, for example, or that can have stories embedded in them?

CHAPTER 3

Where the physical and the digital meet

In the previous chapter I described some of the positive attributes of physical objects and of digital things. I did this in a way that was quite absolute, deliberately isolating the physical from the digital and vice versa. This separation is less and less realistic. Digital and physical things are merging as we create more technological objects and as we embed digital properties into physical things that were inert before.

Indeed it's conceptually difficult for many of us to separate the two in the devices we own. Even though digital items aren't real in a material sense, we still often treat them as such. In our research, for example, we talked to a family that has a specific iPod on which they keep their music for Christmas. Even though that music also lives on a PC somewhere and could be duplicated amongst many devices, the owners of the iPod think of the songs as living on this device. If they want to play festive music, they use it alone, and it serves no other purpose.

To those of us who are used to the fluidity of digital things, this may seem odd, but to many, thinking of these files this way does seem more straightforward than having to conceptually understand that the content can live in many places and can be managed in many ways. There's a reassurance for many people in knowing the physical location of a file, in being able to point to where it is, for example, rather than having to worry about the stability of all the places it could possibly be.

Given that people find it straightforward to think of digital things as living in a particular physical place, is it possible that we're not exploiting that relationship enough? Although devices like PCs have many of the positive attributes of physical things, we don't tend to think of technology like this as sentimental. Computers often have a sense of anonymity. We tend to hide them away. As a container, one computer could easily replace another, much like the cardboard box in which we keep old photos. We feel this way despite the fact that they now often contain some of our most precious memories.

Many pieces of physical technology feel utilitarian in this way, and they seem to underutilize the rich attributes of the digital content that they contain. Digital photo frames, for example, do little but mimic the physical equivalent, showing one image after another without drawing on the rich interactivity, context, and storytelling capacity that could be available to them because of their content.

These physical/digital objects also fail to mine the potential of richer material forms and choices, displaying instead their technological qualities as prominently as possible. To use the same example, digital photo frames are often designed to look like technological objects, drawing attention to themselves, in contrast to traditional photo frames, which recede into the background of our homes. They are made from modern technological materials and usually feature a prominent manufacturer's logo on their front. In this sense they are treated more like televisions, self-consciously projecting their digital qualities, rather than objects that form part of the background fabric of our homes. As technological objects they do little to tell us anything about their content. Their form is technological, but this form is not driven by the digital content within. The digital and physical qualities of these types of items remain disconnected. The frames remain as anonymous as a PC, which seems a missed opportunity because the object's content is often incredibly meaningful.

That's not to say that all technological objects are as anonymous as the everyday computer and the digital photo frame. Mobile phones, for example, don't feel quite as unengaging. They are more personal objects that live on us and with us. We spend time with them and play with them in our spare moments. We personalize them, buying cases for them and applying stickers to them. Through these means they can become more unique and bound to us. These are technological objects that we could start treasuring and feeling sentimental about, that have some of the positive aspects of physical objects that I outlined in the previous chapter.

Bringing the physical and digital closer together

Figure 3-1 is a tongue-in-cheek sketch of what it might be like to inherit a technological object from a deceased relative. It shows an old MP3 player (another type of device that can feel quite personal to us) that has been inherited and put on display like a precious, fragile heirloom. Let's imagine it was used by your grandfather, for example, and has now come to you.

Figure 3-1 Inheriting your grandfather's MP3 player.

What would you feel about this object if you inherited it? Would there be value to you in the physical device simply because it belonged to your grandfather and was used and held by him? Would there be value in the digital content because the music the device contains might tell you something about your grandfather's tastes? Or would the object as a whole lack sentimental value for you?

I'd like to think that both the physical and digital aspects of technological objects like this MP3 player can have sentimental value and that their combination can make that sentiment deeper. There is, after all, a symbiotic relationship between content and container, between the digital and the physical, which can occur naturally. Mobile phones can start to feel more personal simply because their content is personal too. If they become containers for intimate text messages and photos, that content can reflect positively on the device it is stored in and make it something we would not want to lose. Is this something we can design for deliberately, though?

Are there ways to think more deeply about the relationship between the physical and digital, playing on some of the attributes of both that I described earlier, in order to make these kind of objects more significant? Can we take some aspects of the materiality and sentimentality of real objects and combine them with the capacity of the digital for new structures and experiences in order to make artifacts that we can more deeply connect with?

Digital containers

I've talked a little about how technological objects like the PC, phone, and MP3 player are containers for digital things. Digital things have to be stored somewhere, but the relationship of physical and digital is often underplayed so that the physical is considered only functionally: "What is required to enable access to the digital?" To explore the bringing together of the digital and physical to create something richer than that, let's start with the most ubiquitous form of digital storage: the hard drive.

Hard drives tend to be quite anonymous even when they're external and actually visible to us. They are slabs of plastic or metal, designed as functional objects, yet they almost always contain content that matters much to us and that is even sentimental for us. Usually there's no way you would know this by looking at them because there's no sign on them of what they contain. They are like the digital photo frame I described earlier, another example of a technological object whose outside is disconnected from the content it holds.

Maybe making the content more visible, surfacing aspects of what's inside, could make us care more for both the physical item and its digital content? Figure 3-2 shows one simple way this might be done: a hard drive that dynamically displays the age of its content. The date of the oldest and most recent items it contains is displayed on its surface. As more items are added to the device, this age range extends. The longer we have the hard drive, the more we have a sense of a growing, historical archive in a way that we could never have with a more anonymous box (that is, with today's boxes). It gives us a sense of our own history and therefore makes the drive and its content more precious to us.

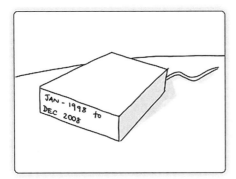

Figure 3-2 A hard drive that shows the age of its content.

This is an example of surfacing the properties of digital content as a part of the material form. Are there also ways of playing with the material aspects of the hard drive alone, in a nondigital way, to get away from its sense of anonymity? Could we create a technological object that more deeply takes advantage of the positive attributes of physical things?

Could an object like a hard drive simply age well, giving us a sense of its history, as many other physical objects do? Figure 3-3 shows a hard drive encased in wood. Like an old wooden school desk with decades of scratches into its surface, it has acquired a patina through use. We think of damage like this to a piece of technology as being a bad thing, but it needn't be. This form of aging can often be what makes a physical thing more dear to us. The nicks and scratches would tell a story of its life as part of a home. Indeed, family members could even be encouraged to scratch their name in its surface as a deliberate act of graffiti that leaves a trail of ownership.

Figure 3-3 A hard drive that ages.

Making digital content part of our environment

To some extent the discussion above is about simple ways of making digital content part of our day-to-day physical environment. This is a key aspect of physical things: they easily become part of our surroundings, and we can put them on display. Showing digital properties on the surface of a hard drive is an attempt to do something similar for digital items, to make them, or aspects of them, part of our surroundings in a way that is more subtle than the technologically self-conscious digital photo frames that are currently representative of physical/digital melding.

There are much richer ways in which digital content can become part of our homes and its rituals through the sensitive design of digital containers. One example of this, which we have built at Microsoft Research Cambridge, is the Digital Slide Viewer. It plays on the idea that one ritual disappearing from our home is the use of physical photos and photo albums to tell stories about places and events to visitors. In the past we could sit around a photo album, or pass around a set of printed photos, as we told others about what they contained. This was an intimate activity that has been made somewhat more awkward during the shift to digital photos by the need to sit around a monitor or laptop to do the same.

The Digital Slide Viewer, shown in Figure 3-4, is an attempt to return some of that intimacy to the act of storytelling. It allows families to store their digital photos on a handheld device that can be passed around in comfort from one family member to another. The device is kept in an attractive storage box that the family can put on display somewhere in their home so that it becomes a part of their environment. When you want to reminisce about some event with visitors, you simply pull the box off a shelf, take out the device, and view and tell stories about what the device shows.

The storage case holds a series of white plastic "slides," each of which can be associated with a set of photos kept on the device. One slide might show all the photos of a recent vacation or of a birthday party. Slides are inserted in the viewer to pull up the associated photos.

The goal of this device is to think of alternatives to the slightly awkward process of showing photos on a PC. It provides an approach that is more elegant than going through folder hierarchies on a laptop. It provides a form that is more socially intimate for the act of reminiscing than the current digital methods.

Figure 3-4 The Digital Slide Viewer.

A history of stories

In the previous chapter I mentioned that one positive aspect of digital things is that they can have their stories and other details embedded in them so that this information isn't lost. These stories can then travel with their digital host as it is duplicated and shared. Physical things have stories associated with them too, of course: who owned them, where they were kept, what happened to them, and so on. Inherited items, particularly, are connected to people, places, and times that are often important to the inheritor. As the object passes through successive generations, however, the stories that keep these details alive can be lost as family members forget to tell them to successive generations.

As the stories are lost, so is an aspect of a family's history, a connection to a shared past. Once the story is gone, the object can become valueless because it is disconnected from the events that gave it meaning.

Are there ways of using digital items as carriers for the stories of physical things? By recording the details of a physical item digitally and connecting the physical and digital together somehow, maybe the stories of these items might be harder to lose and the items could remain valuable to families.

There has been a lot of exploration of different techniques for associating a physical object with a digital file to connect an artifact with a virtual place within which the artifact's stories and history can be stored. Technological objects like phones and PCs have a place within them in which such details can be kept. However, the majority of physical items in our lives don't have this potential, so primary questions include how the physical objects should be "interrogated" to get access to these details and where the digital files should reside.

Tales of Things, for example, is a collaboration between a number of universities in the UK that provides a generic platform for associating digital and physical things. It allows you to print out a special barcode that you can then attach to any physical item. Software installed on a phone can scan the barcode using its built-in camera, decode it, and then go off to the Internet and fetch details about the item that the code is attached to.

This system has been used to track the history of items of clothing donated to a goodwill shop so that new buyers can get a sense of where it came from and who owned it previously. (See Figure 3-5.) It has been used to attach codes to public works of art so that viewers can find out more about what they're looking at. It's not a stretch to also imagine a system like this being used to record stories about an heirloom before it is passed down through the family. As long as the code stayed with the item the family would have some way besides oral history of reminding themselves of the heirloom's past.

Figure 3-5 Tales of Things. A tag on a secondhand piece of jewelry tells you more about the item's history.

Similarly, BookCrossing is a service that allows you to release a book "into the wild" and track where it went, who read it, and so on. It simply requires you to print out a label with a unique identifier on it (shown in Figure 3-6), stick that in the front of the book, and give the book away (or place it somewhere that a stranger might find it). Once someone finds the book, the person follows the instructions on the label, types the ID into the BookCrossing website, and leaves some details about what has happened to the item. The site gradually builds up a history of this book's travels. Again, it's not hard to imagine this system in the context of heirlooms, with successive generations adding new layers of stories to an item.

Systems like Tales of Things and BookCrossing could also be used to draw together sets of inherited items rather than just individual ones. Often when someone passes away, objects that are part of a broader collection that has been assembled throughout a life are passed along. This could happen in a haphazard way, like a library of books accrued over a lifetime, or it could be more deliberate, like my collection of transistor radios I mentioned in Chapter 2, a collection of items I've specifically sought out.

Figure 3-6 A BookCrossing label.

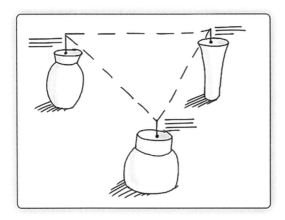

Figure 3-7 Items that used to be part of a collection, connected together digitally.

Such collections are often disassembled as the items are distributed amongst different family members. The items' association with one another as part of a set is then lost. Digital files could be used to keep this connection so that although the items are no longer physically collocated, they could still be associated with one another. Scanning a barcode (like those used in Tales of Things) might bring up the connections from one item to the photos and stories of the rest of the items in the original collections, as shown in Figure 3-7.

Exchanging state

In bringing the physical and digital more closely together, I've talked so far about tightening the connections between the two, surfacing digital properties in the material form and associating digital and physical things together. What about an actual exchange of state? What might it mean for a digital thing to become physical and a physical thing digital?

Described this way the idea seems odd, but this isn't as absurd a notion as it sounds. We print digital content all the time, for example, manifesting it as an object that will from then on age and deteriorate as all physical things do. We take photos of physical things, too, preserving them in digital form. They can't be experienced like the original, but they provide a record and a trigger for reminiscing.

Following are some compelling examples of projects that explore the transition from digital into physical more deeply. Each plays on the positive attributes of physical items that a digital thing inherits when it becomes "real," and each attempts to make something new and precious.

Christopher R. Weingarten is a music journalist in the United States who vowed to write 1,000 reviews of new music releases over the course of 2009, all on the microblogging site Twitter. Having duly succeeded in his task, he released a limited edition wooden box containing every tweet, individually hand-typed on index cards. (See Figure 3-8.) It is described as a "physical representation of Twitter." Because the box was released in a limited edition of 30 with an emphasis on hand-crafting, it feels clear that the goal was to create something exclusive and precious from a source that is disposable and viewable by anyone.

Similarly, the company FigurePrints offers players of the online game World of Warcraft the ability to take their "avatar"—the character in the game that represents them—and produce it as a material object in full color. (See Figure 3-9 for an example.) By doing this players get a fully manifested artifact that represents their investment in the game. It becomes something they can put on display, which acts as a singular reminder of a world locked away in a machine.

Figure 3-8 @1000TimesYes card.

Figure 3-9 "Wreker," a character printed out by FigurePrints.

These are examples of digital content made physical. Each item acts as a record of an event or experience that has sentimental value to its creator. By making these digital moments and things physical, the digital is frozen in state so that even as the digital content is over-whelmed—by a deluge of new tweets in the case of the Twitter box and by new gaming experiences or equipment in the case of the avatar—the items preserve some point in time. Both the box of tweets and the avatar statue act as objects that sentimentally reconnect a person with a specific digital experience at a specific moment in time. As such they become as rich a representation of a person's life as any other object and could become a new form of heirloom.

At Microsoft Research Cambridge we also see value in the reverse, in creating digital versions of physical things. Once an object is recorded digitally, we can exploit some of the positive attributes of digital things. We can use the digital version as a means of sharing an item with people who can't be physically collocated with us, for example. The digital version can also become part of the soup of digital photos and act similarly, as a serendipitous reminder of our past. This is something we played with in the design our Family Archive system, shown in Figure 3-10.

Figure 3-10 Family archive showing a pair of scanned clogs from a vacation to Holland.

When we bring objects home with us from our vacations or merely from our moving through the world, these objects connect us with the time we spent away. We might bring shells home from the beach to remind of us of a day spent by the sea. With the shift to digital photography, we have to deal separately with the digital and the physical when it comes to reminiscing because they exist in such different states. Whereas in the past we might have put our printed photos with the shells on a shelf, in one combined record of our day by the sea, now they live in separate spaces, one physical and the other virtual. Family Archive is a system that allows family members to store all their digital photos in one piece of furniture in their home; it acts as a central, visible repository for the family's shared history that can encourage reminiscence. An important part of the system is a built-in camera, which takes photos of physical things so that they can also be stored digitally. Souvenirs from a vacation can be stored with the photos from the same trip, and this allows for reminiscing that includes both.

In this chapter I've talked a little about opportunities for understanding and exploiting the positive attributes of the digital and physical in order to make new representations of what we value. A recurring theme that I haven't been explicit about is how our relationship with items we value changes with time and perspective. Our views change over a lifetime, and with them so too does our attitude towards the things we own and inherit. In Chapter 4, "Our digital lifespan," I'll consider some ways in which our relationship to technology and reminiscing change as we age.

Design challenges

In Chapter 2, the design challenges concerned the exchange of properties between physical and digital artifacts. Here I'd like you to consider what it means to merge their properties so that digital things can complement the physical and vice versa.

→ How might we design physical containers for digital things to materially reflect the value of their digital content on their surface so as to make us more aware of how important those things are to us?

→ How might we design a system that connects digital content to inert physical objects in order for those objects' histories to persist and their heirloom status to be extended?

→ If we made digital things physical and physical things digital, how might we treasure them differently?

PART II

A digital life

I N THE INTRODUCTION to Part I, "Stuff and sentimentality," I talked a little about the experience I had going through my grandfather's old photos after he passed away. They told me a little about the life he'd led, gave me a sense of what seemed to matter to him, and allowed me to reflect on how our experience of reminiscing through sentimental artifacts in the future will be different from the one I had with his artifacts because of the ways digital things are inherently different from physical things.

I might have implied that my grandfather didn't do any reminiscing of his own during his lifetime, that the only access I had to his past was through his things, but that is of course not true. It's human nature to think and talk about the past with others, and he wasn't different in this respect. He did think about his past and talk about his experiences as a pilot, for example, while he was alive. My impression, though, is that he rarely did this until he started to get quite elderly. As a "younger man" (but still after retirement) he'd kept his focus on what was going on in his immediate life, and his reminiscing was of his more recent history. It was only once his world started to close a little, with some loss of mobility and eyesight, that he spent more time with his memories and went further back. Once the present became less accessible, the past became a more interesting place to visit.

In this part I want to look more closely at how the structure or phases of our lives might affect the kind of content we want to keep for sentimental reasons and the amount of reminiscing we do with that content. First I'll discuss this in terms of a life, and then I'll talk a little about the impact of bereavement and the process of death in terms of how it changes the way we look back on someone else's past.

CHAPTER 4

Our digital lifespan

My plan with this chapter is to talk about some specific phases of our lives in the context of looking back. At the outset of this book I stated that my goal was to talk about some of the changes that might come about in the way we reminisce as we shift to preserving our lives digitally, so it seems important that we have a sense of when reminiscing is important throughout our lives and what it is we might be reminiscing about.

For example, I'll talk about how becoming a parent results in a burgeoning of content as a child's life becomes the focus for a lot of photography, videography, and so on. These sorts of big landmarks, like getting married, are all important events and starts of phases on which we typically want to reflect later in life, and they form a common record of our past that can be recognized by others as being part of the way their lives are structured, too. When we meet with others who have had similar experiences, we can exchange stories with them and compare notes.

I fully acknowledge that these phases and experiences aren't common (or even desirable) for everyone. In a lot of ways they're the cliché of a "normal" life. Bear with me, though. To some extent this will be an exercise in stereotyping that I hope we can get past. I'm going to be unabashedly UK- or US-centric too, which may get annoying if those aren't the cultures that you're familiar with. These are the cultures that I've experienced, however, and that I can use as examples to support my key points. This chapter isn't about the details that I describe, really. It's about highlighting that our lives have ups and downs. At different points we have different relationships with the past, and artifacts play different roles in remembrance because of that.

As you're reading this chapter, think about your own personal experiences, the phases of the lives around you, and key moments that matter. Think about the things you do to try to preserve those moments, the objects you keep, the photos you take, and so on.

There are many reasons why people choose to preserve items throughout their lifespan. Some of these are sentimental (which is the primary focus of this book). Artifacts play a lot of other roles when it comes to memory, however. Abigail Sellen at Microsoft Research Cambridge likes to describe motives for preserving artifacts of memory as the "5 Rs." These include **Reminiscing**, or looking back on the past for primarily emotional or sentimental reasons. Similarly, **Reflecting** is a process through which people can gain new insights or perspectives on the past through the examination of patterns of experience. Slightly more mundane than this is **Recollecting**, which concerns the act of remembering past details of an event, often for practical purposes (remembering where you left your car keys, for example). **Retrieving**, also involves the act of finding facts, information or objects from the past. It is like recollecting, but includes deduction or inference as alternative strategies, using associations between memories to help find answers. Finally, **Remembering** intentions is a form of prospective memory through which people plan future activities. This is the act through which people might remember to run errands, for example.

It's interesting to consider in the following section how some of these aspects of life overlap. How, for example, items we kept for mundane reasons, like notes we wrote to ourselves to remember to do a task, can change nature if we keep them. Guest lists we wrote when planning a wedding, for example, can change from being mundane tools for arranging an event to objects that allow us to reminisce about the event itself, in this case helping us remember the participants.

Infants

In our examination of the specific phases of our lives about which we're sentimental and during which we look back, let's begin at the beginning, with infancy.

Recording a life

I've had a digital camera since well before my daughter was born. Before her birth I used it primarily to try to capture and keep in memory the places I visited on my travels. I'm a fan of modern architecture, so I often spent time taking photos of buildings I admired. I got into night shooting, too, capturing the trails of car lights in the darkness.

Since my daughter was born towards the end of 2005, I feel like her life has become my main photo subject. As my daughter's birth approached and passed, the subject of my shots changed radically. I focused the lenses of a series of video and still cameras in her direction. Since then she has been the subject of one long exercise in the recording of significant and insignificant (or temporarily insignificant?) moments.

I'm grateful for my daughter's patience as she's come to understand what it means to have a camera pointed at her. She's even developed a fake smile to use when I ask her to pose. I would feel like my recording activities were a little extreme, except that as I look around me at all the other parents I spend time with I can see that they are doing exactly the same as me, taking a near constant stream of photos and video of their offspring. They feel the need to capture many if not most of their child's experiences, just as I do. Children's parties, for example, rarely end without a group photo, lining up all the kids present, the adults jostling to get their child's eyes pointed in their direction.

I suspect there are probably a lot of reasons why parents feel this need. It's an amazing thing to watch someone develop at such a fast pace, biologically and intellectually, when you're used to your own more sedentary changes. There's a sense that you are literally watching time pass before your eyes as this person develops from an infant to a toddler in a matter of months. As they learn to eat, to walk, to talk, these actions that seem so mundane to an adult become more significant, somehow, as you watch someone come to grips with these actions for the first time. Recording all of this becomes a form of documentary creation, a way of doing stop-motion over time, with the ability to compare old photos with new as a child develops.

My sense is that these photos and videos are being taken not only as a personal recording, for the parent themselves, but also on behalf of others. In his work on why people keep sentimental artifacts, my colleague David Kirk describes three key recipients for whom objects are kept: for the owner themselves; for a "known other," such as a family member or, in the case of my photos, for my daughter; and for an "unknown other," as a form of legacy in which the recipient is not known. Capturing the development of a child has a sense of all three. I feel like I'm taking photos of my daughter for my own future reminiscing. I also feel like I'm taking them on her behalf for her to have a record of herself that I'll bequeath to her one day. I'm also potentially taking them for an "unknown other," perhaps for her family if she has one, so that they have a record of their parent when they want one.

A process of self-reflection

So children's lives are endlessly recorded. What happens to all this content, though? Not a lot, it seems. Many items just sit in a folder on a hard drive, forgotten for the moment. Typically it is only a small set of these items that are actually acted upon: edited and shared with others, for example.

Some items are used to create new kinds of artifacts that celebrate all this change. Many parents, for example, create baby books that log their child's development, recording the changes in this person speaking and walking for the first time, making friends and visiting new places. These changes are supported by a record of photos, cut out and pasted next to the facts. The creation of these books isn't a new activity. My wife has the baby book that her mother meticulously created about her, and I have mine. Figure 4-1 shows my daughter's baby book.

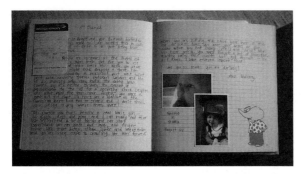

Figure 4-1 My daughter's baby book.

You will note that my wife and I have these books that are about us. Somehow these books have ended up in our hands, given to us by our parents. It seems a little odd that our parents haven't kept them to support their memory of our development but instead have insisted that we have them. Perhaps we have ended up with them because we went looking for them once we'd had our own child. Once we'd started to create a record of her, we wondered where the record of us had gone.

As a parent, the act of recording a life exposes us to a lot of opportunity for self-reflection. By watching someone else develop, we wonder how we ourselves developed. Similarly, by simply making decisions about how we parent on a day-to-day basis, we wonder how our own parents made similar decisions.

This act of recording another can make us seek out records of ourselves when we were children. We might do this simply to compare our physiology, to see whether we looked the same as infants as our children do now. Maybe this is the point in time that our own parents were always hoping for, when the artifacts that they created about us and for us reemerge and fulfill some of their original intentions as time capsules of development.

One thing that having a child does is allow you to reflect on your own childhood. In taking responsibility for bringing someone else up, you also wonder how you yourself were raised. When trying to decide how to tackle questions of routine or strategies for dinner or bedtime, questions are inevitably raised about how your own parents decided their approach to parenting you. Both my wife and I have found that our parents have a great deal of amnesia when it comes to their own recollections of their parental choices. It seems ironic that despite all the recording they did of us, they have lost some of the capacity to remember their own actions and decisions from the point in time when these records were made.

Celebrating through recording

I'm not sure why our parents made these baby books of us or what they expected to happen to them. They are not just a record of a person's life but are a celebration of it, of moments that matter and goals achieved. The same is true of many photo albums, which form a powerful and (hopefully) lasting record of a life that will mature and evolve. They play a dual role: as both a record of a person or event and as a form of celebration.

Richard Harper, one of my colleagues at Microsoft Research Cambridge, argues that the taking of photos used to be primarily an act of recording, about making a record of a moment in time. Now that digital cameras are ubiquitous and embedded in our phones, the nature of the photo-taking act has changed. I was recently at a concert in a large stadium, and looking around me I could see thousands of small displays, lit up in the dark, as audience members recorded the event. Richard argues that this is a form of celebration of the event, that fans in the audience were demonstrating their participation by all taking photos together. The output of those images is almost irrelevant compared to what the act says about the commitment of the image maker to that moment (or that band). Perhaps this is true of the baby book, too, or of the act of recording a child's development more generally—it is in some way a celebration of parenthood.

This act of recording is rarely sustained, though. It's common that entries in a baby book gradually dry up, and a second child often does not have the same level of observation applied to them as the first. Perhaps this indicates that the novelty of the experience of childhood for the parent subsides, that watching a second child develop simply (if unfairly) isn't as interesting the second time around. Maybe as a child's pace of development slows and gets more subtle, as the years of rapid change, of learning to walk and talk within a matter of years, give way to slower progress, the milestones spread out and it becomes a struggle to maintain the routine of recording. It's also possible that at a certain age this constant observation simply gets invasive. As the character of the individual grows and the child's self-consciousness and sense of personal space also grow, it starts to feel more and more inappropriate to point a camera at them continuously.

Passing on experiences

It is not just the images we take, or the things we make, that play a role as a record of children and childhood. Often, physical artifacts are kept to tie us to moments in our children's lives. We might preserve clothes that we particularly associate them with, which might act as reminders not just of specific periods in time, but also give us some sense of scale, to remind us how small our baby once was. Similarly, we might keep other toys that our child played with or loved the most. These tie us back to specific moments and carry with them physical attributes through touch, smell, and scale that a photo or video cannot.

My wife and I both have lots of items that our parents preserved from our childhood, and many of them have ended up in the hands of our daughter. She plays with an old dolls house built for my wife by her father, for example. They are an odd form of heirloom in that they still have utility, they are sentimental to us, and they could become sentimental to our child. These are lucky objects—most items from our childhood were not so fortunate and long ago were discarded.

We often still have strong memories of things we played with as children, even though they have long since disappeared. These are things that we wish our child could experience. In many of these cases, though, it isn't actually important that we have the original. What matters is that there is some way for us to pass on the experience, the same sense of thrill (hopefully) of the original, and if we have to use something similar, then so be it. What we are in effect interested in trying to do is bequeath an experience of our childhood rather than an artifact of it.

My wife and I have both remembered toys from our childhood that we loved, which we have subsequently sought out on eBay and bought for our daughter. It mattered to us that the toys were the same or similar model to the ones we played with and that they were of a similar age. It mattered far less that they were literally the same object. Our daughter could have a experience of them, we hoped, similar to the one we treasured in our memories. In this sense, eBay and sites like it are an incredible resource for the re-creation of past experiences, with page after page of old toys and memorabilia.

It's not just physical items from our childhood that we can foist on our daughter. My wife and I also both watched Sesame Street as children, and we've been keen to expose her to it. We think of it, as well as the other shows that we experienced when young, as being the "best" because it is inherently part of being a parent that contemporary childhood things seem thin and valueless. The things we experienced in our childhood were naturally richer and more worthwhile. (It's probably quite common that parents feel that the shows through which they were educated or entertained when little were more effective than the contemporary equivalents they now see around them. I doubt this is true and consider this phenomenon as a form of sentimental filtering.)

To give our daughter the experience we had of Sesame Street, we found rereleases of early episodes of the show. I'm not actually sure if they are the same ones that I actually saw as a child, but they correspond to the time when I was watching. Again, like the items bought on eBay, some of the specifics don't matter. What we want is a re-creation of a sense of the experience we had when watching ourselves. The shows we bought come on a DVD in a box marked "Old School," a term which seems to be designed both as a celebration of the authenticity of the content and a slightly stinging reminder of our age. These are shows that are 40 years old yet are stored on the most modern technology. This contradiction doesn't matter to my wife and me—we're not trying to pass on an original recording of the show. We're trying to give our daughter a sense of the experience we had. Increasingly, many of these experiences are not just on DVD anymore but are also on sites like YouTube. Like many things today, this content is all just a click away.

Growing up

Reminiscing begins to change radically when the period being recorded or reflected upon is no longer infancy.

Social centers and personal space

Earlier I talked about the volume of recording that many babies and toddlers are subject to as they develop. I mentioned that one possible reason that parents start to reduce the amount of recording is that as a child grows older his or her sense of self and self-consciousness increases. Many older children simply dislike being the subject of a photograph. Older children and teens cease to be quite the center of sentimental activity they once were as the recording of their life slows. Instead they start to develop their own sense of and relationship to memory generally and their own past in particular.

As many of us have experienced, visiting our own past can actually be deeply embarrassing to us when we are young. This is perhaps a phase we build up to as we reach adolescence. When my daughter was very young, she was fascinated by pictures of herself as a baby but unable to understand that they were portraits of her. She now understands this and continues to be interested in the images. She is five and not yet particularly self-conscious. But as we age many things can become deeply embarrassing to us. Many adolescents would rather not think of themselves as having once been a baby, and I have seen many parents use the threat of getting out a baby book (usually in jest) to elicit a reaction.

Part of this comes about through a more conscious sense of self and how we are perceived by others as social centers shift from family to friends, particularly as more time is spent at school. What friends think and what friends are doing can become far more critical an issue to many young people than what their family is doing or thinks of them.

It's not just social centers that change. Our relationship to space changes, too, as we grow older. More priority is placed on personal space, as well as ownership of some of the space around us. Bedrooms become a place that we "own," can personalize, and into which many of us can retreat. We often have very strong memories of these spaces that we created for ourselves and personalized to reflect our insights and the way we wished to be perceived. Many of us remember the posters we hung on the walls of our bedrooms as young adults, for example.

In his work on the virtual possessions of teenagers, Will Odom, a social scientist and designer who has spent a lot of time with my team in Cambridge, describes how "the display and organization of possessions in teenagers' bedrooms play significant roles in shaping their evolving sense of self. The presentation of trophies, photo collages, and posters of popular culture icons, among other things, shape teens' perceptions of who they are and who they might become. In this way, the bedroom presents a material infrastructure that teenagers can exert control over in order to experiment with their identity." This sense of identity is defined socially, too, through friends who also play a role as record-keepers of past events too. This activity no longer takes place just physically, but virtually, too. Will observed how, for some of his subjects, an event didn't become "real" or "authentic" until the photos taken at it had been through the process of being shared, tagged, triaged and commented on with friends.

This shift in social center from family to friends can impact technological use in the home, of course, particularly with objects that are intended to bring families closer together. Many of the devices we've created to explore issues of family communication or shared history, for example, are intended to be used by all family members together, rather than just one individual. Our Family Archive system (mentioned earlier and shown in Figure 3-10) is a piece of furniture into which all family members can put their digital photos and videos and into which they can scan physical artifacts that they want to remember later. When we've deployed systems like this, we've found that the very young are keen to engage with what we've built and keen to participate and play with it. They spend time exploring it and making it do things we never intended. But older children often participate less; they see it as something not intended for them. Some of this response seems to come about because the family is less of a focus for them than their friends.

Taking on the responsibility of recording

Not all reminiscing is anathema for the young, though. Many young people start taking on some responsibility for their own past, as they start their own diaries or, increasingly, record and share their thoughts and experiences with their friends. A lot of this now happens online, in the glare of social networks. I wonder how this recent shift, from recording our own lives intimately and within a small group, to sharing broadly by default, changes the nature of the kind of content the young might create. It's hard to imagine writing a diary without having some sense in the back of your mind of who or when it will be read and how it is a form of time-capsule to your past or even a legacy to others. I suspect that a lot of the online activity driven by the young isn't thought of in terms of the past. It isn't posted or shared with the idea that it will also become a record of or connection to another time. Perhaps that isn't surprising. Reminiscing, in this sense, is something to be explored in the short term (like sharing photos with friends after a concert as a form of celebration of that event) rather than the long.

Taking technology for granted

Of course, another key differentiator for the young is the ease with which they live with new technology. Some of this may be a result of the speed at which they learn and the fearless way in which they can push technology to its limits. Their lack of a frame of reference for a technological past is key to this. The growth in new technologies and services through which we can share and experience content, enabled particularly by the personal computer, the Internet, and the phone, still seems rapid and novel to me. For children it is all they have ever known.

I grew up in the technological transition of audio media from the LP through tapes and CDs and now to downloads. Naturally, I miss aspects of former forms of media, like album art or the feeling of turning an LP over (or even just the concept of an A side and a B side that a record has). Each generation resets this sense of technological sentimentality as they lose those connections with past forms and experiences. I might try to give my daughter a sense of what it was like to play an LP—indeed I own a beautiful old player I could use for this—but I suspect it would be a bewildering oddity compared to the ease with which she can pop in a CD or hit play on a digital music player.

Perhaps, then, some technological sentimentality of the form described above is unavoidable. Whenever new technology takes over old, novel features are enabled that can often be very liberating. At the same time some positive attributes of the old equipment are lost. I remember, for example, playing my first CD. The experience of simply pressing the "next" button on the player to skip to the subsequent song seemed magic. Gone was the pain of fast-forwarding and stopping a tape player repeatedly to try to find the gap between songs. Yet suddenly the ritual of creating mix tapes was gone, something I still miss to this day.

Since technology changes so rapidly, such losses can be associated with specific generations. Older generations don't have the same sense of sentimentality I have for creating mix tapes, because tapes were a technology that replaced what they experienced. And subsequent generations listen with bewilderment to descriptions of what we used to go through to do the simplest task.

Sentimental adolescence

Interestingly, as adults there is some question about the authenticity of our memories of adolescence or indeed of our past more generally. (Let's set aside for a second the reality of an adolescent's sentimentality.) This period of our lifespan is often one that we are given to reflect on more than much of the rest of our life. The Reminiscence Bump, one form of cognitive bias (a deviation in our judgment from the expected), describes how middle and older adults have a tendency to recall more from their adolescence and early adulthood (between the ages of about 10 to 25) than they do from much of the rest of their life. Our memories of this period are somehow stronger.

Similarly, Rosy Retrospection is another form of bias that describes our tendency to see our past in a way that is more positive than it actually was. This might, for example, predispose adults to see their youth through rose-tinted spectacles.

We have a tendency, therefore, to put more emphasis on, and have more resonance with, our youth than perhaps we should, proportionally to the whole of our lifespan. Trusting in the reminiscences about our young lives should be done with some caution. It's hard to remember what it was really like growing up.

Adults

As we grow older the patterns of independence started as an adolescent continue and solidify.

Changing phases

Independence starting with adolescence continues until eventually we move away from our parents and find homes of our own. This is a big change, obviously, and a huge personal responsibility. Homes can be a liability or an asset, but from a material perspective they provide new surfaces on which to extend and reflect ourselves. They are nests to be occupied and lined with the things we already own, as well as with new things.

The large changes we make as we get older, such as leaving home, graduating from college, starting a career, or getting married, push us to make choices about our relationship with the past through our material possessions. At each of these points decisions have to be made about the things we own. We decide what we will leave behind or take with us, what we will keep and what we will discard, and what we will archive or put on display.

Technology can provide odd connections back through these changes. Steve Hodges, another colleague of mine at Microsoft Research Cambridge, literally shut the lid on the laptop he was using at college once he'd submitted his thesis and was done with that phase of his education. He was on to bigger and better things, starting a career. He kept the device, though, as a form of archive. He recently turned that laptop back on again, after 20 years, and was surprised to see that it actually started up and that everything on screen was exactly where he had left it. In some ways it provided a window for him back to his college years in a way not possible with photos.

Sharing history

Many of us eventually choose to share our lives with another person. We might live together or even get married, for example. This intermingling of lives creates a big shift in terms of sentimentality and artifacts. Two people bring together their memories and things, mixing them in one space. This can be a comfortable or uncomfortable experience. The home can become a negotiated space, owned by one or other of the couple and made up of objects that have meaning to that individual, or artifacts can comingle. As time passes, a home shared by two people is filled with objects that belong to both, associated with memories that are shared. Figure 4-2 shows a simple example.

Bringing together digital assets can be a far more complicated issue than the combining of physical assets. Computers and online services have layers of identity, security, purchase history, and so on that constantly emphasize the individual. When two people combine their collections of physical books they can be arranged together and exchanged. The current state of digital book purchasing, which focuses on single accounts, makes the equivalent virtual experience virtually impossible. My wife and I have to share the same Amazon Kindle account, for example, in order to read and swap books with one another. The alternative is to buy two copies of anything we both want to read. Amazon has actually been quite open-minded in creating a system for digital book lending, but it limits the period of the loan to

14 days. The idea of setting any limit seems odd after experiencing the flexibility of physical books.

Children bring another layer of artifacts and reminiscence to the home. I talked quite a bit about this earlier on from the perspective of recording and preserving the development of a child, but children, of course, also have an impact on the space around the family and change the nature of what it means to say "we" instead of "I." It is not merely that these new little people arrive, of course. Roles are redefined as adults become parents too, and the home becomes representative of this group of people, of families as well as individuals.

Figure 4-2 A family portrait.

Seniors

Later in life there's often a change of scale, a sense of resizing for parents, and a sense of refocusing for parents and nonparents alike.

Emptying the nest

Eventually children leave home. For the parents left behind, it's common for them to find their home, formerly full to the brim and chaotic, now a place that echoes with unused space. Sentimental objects can take on additional poignancy. Photos of children, for example, can serve to remind parents not only of their children when they were younger but also of their current absence from the home.

When children leave home, they don't take everything with them, of course. Parents are often left to deal with the artifacts of childhood. Things that the children left behind have to be sorted through and kept, passed on to their former owners, or discarded. These artifacts are a little ambiguous about their ownership. My mother still has a few items of mine in her loft; she sees these items as very much belonging to me. I think she finds it a little annoying that I still haven't taken charge of them, but I quite like the idea that they still live in her home. I suspect that deep down she does, too.

Parents deal with this change in the nature of their home in different ways. Some find new uses for old bedrooms, which become offices, studios, or gyms, spaces of opportunity and new interests. Some parents don't change these spaces at all but preserve them in the state in which they were left. Perhaps they don't want to deal with this change or simply like the idea that their offspring have somewhere familiar to sleep when they come home. Often parents find their homes have changed so much with the departure that they feel it is time for a change of place themselves, so they move to somewhere new. Perhaps they felt that their home simply didn't feel the same anymore. Maybe they just feel they had too much space to deal with once their children left.

For a child revisiting the family home after moving out, any of these changes can feel jarring. Whether the parents reuse their old bedrooms, preserve them, or move wholesale to a new location, the experience of the past through the experience of a place changes significantly.

Reflecting on life

I've talked to a number of people who have had what I call the "uncomfortable conversation." One day, when you are visiting your parents' home, you are asked, "So, what do you want after I die?" I'm not entirely sure what triggers this conversation. Perhaps it happens when the child leaves home, perhaps at the parents' retirement. It might happen at some point when the parents start getting more conscious of their own mortality, perhaps after illness, for example. There seems to be a stoic quality to this conversation, from the parents' side, with a "matter of fact" air to it. Children are often shocked by it, however, since it can be the first time that they've considered their parents' mortality.

According to the conversations I've had with people who have experienced this, what the children tell their parents is sentimental to them can often surprise their parents. There is a disconnect, perhaps, between the memories of childhood and what stands out for each of them. Perhaps it is to be expected that the events that stand out for the parents are not the same as those that stand out for the child.

Old age often becomes a period of personal reflection, a time at which to take stock on a life. As I mentioned earlier, my grandfather didn't really start exploring his memories until he was quite old. He reached a point at which his past became more important, and the artifacts he had from it did the same. He surrounded himself more with them. My impression is that this is quite common and natural, that seniors often spend more time with their memories than they did when younger.

Tied up with this are issues of legacy, of planning to pass on both artifacts and the stories of a lifetime. In Chapter 5, "A digital death," I'll discuss the sensitive but important process through which objects and memories change hands from one generation to the next.

Design challenges

Inevitably with this chapter a number of challenges concern the simple transition of time.

→ How might we design systems that allow us to see how someone changes with time?

→ What might the digital equivalent of the baby book be like?

→ What are more lightweight ways in which we might keep a record of our family that don't have the pressure that photography can have?

→ How might we design experiences that retain the positive attributes of old technology in new?

There are also opportunities in thinking about easing tough transitions in our life.

→ How might we design systems that help anticipate the new phases in our life and help prepare us for these big changes?

→ How might we design systems that make the transition of social center from the home to friends an easier one for both teenagers and their family?

→ How might we design ways that allow two people to bring together and combine their digital things as easily as their physical?

→ How might we design ways that allow parents to clear out or archive their child's digital things when they leave home?

We could also explore what it means to think about our past in terms of phases.

→ How might we design experiences that allow us to more easily recall and share the important things from specific parts of our younger lives?

CHAPTER 5

A digital death

Death is clearly a somber topic and not one that the digital industry has had to come to terms with in the past. Technology tends to put an emphasis on newness and freshness, and issues of bereavement have seemed out of place when thinking about our digital experiences. It is a sign of the maturity of the digital age—how long we've spent simply living with computers, for example—that issues around legacy are starting to come to the fore. When our friends and family die, they are now leaving traces of themselves in 1s and 0s, as well as in the physical forms we would expect. Their legacy now includes technological objects (phones, laptops, and so on) and their contents (files and folders). Increasingly, it also includes content stored elsewhere, a footprint of their online life, left through the sites and services they used when alive.

My grandfather didn't leave any digital traces of himself. He left things that I was able to digitize and share, such as photos, which are not the same thing. He left some media, recorded onto magnetic tape, but I wouldn't argue that this is digital, although you could argue it is technological, in the same way that an LP record is.

One treasured item I have from him is a recording made for BBC Radio from the cockpit of an aircraft he was flying. Over the drone of the engines you can hear his clipped English accent talking about the handling of the plane to the program's presenter. This recording is something that I've digitized. It is now an MP3 file, a form that promises flexibility and security, but which means that it sits rather anachronistically next to the songs and albums I listen to on my laptop. Now I have to put effort into making sure that this sentimental recording doesn't turn up in some randomly selected list of songs that I might play when jogging.

When my father passed away in 2010, I had more digital items to deal with. During the last decade of his life, he sent email, browsed the web, took digital photos, and did many of the other activities we now take for granted. He left a laptop and a PC in his cottage and, like the rest of his belongings, we had to decide what to do with them. The laptop had been recently formatted and was empty of personal content. The PC was in a pretty awful state, externally, and not something I wanted to preserve, so rather than keeping the whole case instead I took the hard drive from its insides and discarded the rest. (See Figure 5-1.) Somehow this has felt a little dishonorable. I've been left with this mysterious technological object whose contents I should at some point explore. At the moment it is in a pile with the physical photos of his family, which he also left behind. Now both the prints and the hard drive are treasured resources that could offer a rich record of his life. The longer I do nothing with them, however, the more they seem reminders of a task not yet undertaken.

In Chapter 4, "Our digital lifespan," I talked a little about some of the intergenerational issues that are also echoed here by the simple differences in technological legacy between what my grandfather left behind and what my father did. As new generations come and go, their relationship with technology changes and their legacies reflect that. In this chapter I want to deal more specifically with the processes in play before, during, and after bereavement, to understand how digital things do or should change hands.

Figure 5-1 My father's hard drive.

A part of due process

The "uncomfortable conversation" mentioned in the previous chapter, in which parents instruct their children to tell them which items in their home they would like to inherit, is perhaps symptomatic of some of the distance we put between ourselves and death. Focusing on material, practical issues, such as the ultimate destination of objects in a home, makes this an easier conversation to have. Most people don't like to think about death, and as a subject it is still quite taboo, but having something pragmatic and specific to address can create a buffer from the reality of bereavement and loss that makes the conversation possible between parents and their children.

There can be many practical steps that are part of the process of planning for the end of our lives. Through wills, for example, we attempt to objectively analyze the extent of our estate and make decisions about how our possessions are distributed. It can be quite a surreal process as it forces you to make very difficult choices that you have never made before. When my daughter was born, for example, my wife and I wrote our wills to give her some security in the event of our deaths. Having to decide which of our various siblings and parents received which items felt like quite a vicious act. We had to be specific and fair, but in the end our possessions didn't divide up neatly, leaving us with the sneaking suspicion that what we'd decided wasn't quite right and never could be.

There were a few buffers in this process that made it easier for us to undertake it while keeping the reality of bereavement a distant one. The first was time—the assumption that our deaths would not occur for years. In this sense the will was a form of insurance rather than something imminent. Perhaps this made the experience of writing it more surreal since it felt speculative. A second buffer came about through the use of a third party, the law firm we worked with, who would reveal the will's contents to our family when necessary. The will could remain hidden, our wishes not acted on, until we were gone. This anonymity meant we didn't have to confront our family more directly with the sensitivity of the topic.

The process of creating a will is currently focused on physical things, on the distribution of assets, the contents of a home, significant family heirlooms, and so on. However, digital things now need to be accommodated as they make up a more significant part of our estate. Digital things can be both sentimental (such as digital photos) and a form of asset (such as an online bank account). Is it possible to deal with these sorts of artifacts within this tradition and process of heredity?

A number of services have emerged that attempt to address this issue. LegacyLocker.com, for example, is a website through which you can store the details and passwords for different digital assets and accounts and even bequeath them to specific beneficiaries. On your death the service can send out digital "letters" to different family members, which can be authored beforehand. This service is intended as a parallel process to the traditional routes of wills and probate.

Deathswitch.com is a site that provides an extreme solution to triggering the distribution of digital assets. After your sign up for its services, it prompts you for a password on a regular basis. If a long period of time passes without you entering one, it automatically starts sending out your digital secrets (passwords to sites, for example) to the beneficiaries that you have defined at the outset.

Similarly, the Wells Fargo bank offers a "digital vault" within which people can store their important assets in digital form. It is intended both for items that are already digital and also for scans of objects (such as passports) that need to be kept secure. Its aim is providing a secure space away from home to preserve items in the event of a fire or loss of the original, but clearly there are questions about how a secure digital place such as this operates as part of a legacy.

MyWonderfulLife.com is a website that focuses on the ritual of death in addition to the more pragmatic issues such as the distribution of property. On the site you can outline the kind of funeral you want and, to some extent, how you want to be memorialized and remembered. It attempts to put you in control of not just your assets but also the memory of yourself that you leave behind.

Although wills are currently a primary mechanism through which we deal with the material aspects of life, these examples above are just a few instances of different solutions for dealing with the digital that are starting to appear online. Some are more practical than others, and it is unclear how most will fit into the tradition of heredity so that we know what to expect when someone passes away. But these sites are not just providing alternative ways of dealing with digital and material legacy; they are also providing alternate outlets for dealing with the more subtle processes of bereavement.

Nonmaterial legacies

There is more to legacy then simply the objects that make up a life. People care about the stories, too, which put the objects in context; people want insights into a life that reflect experience and memory. Time needs to be set aside to draw out these tales, though, and this is a task that never seems a high enough priority and is often left too late. Despite all that my grandfather left behind, I regret not taking the time to sit down with him to hear and even record the stories behind the objects he left behind. I think that feeling is quite common, the sense of losing a connection back through time. Memories of ancestors that the deceased knew when they were young, for example, will be lost and, therefore, so will connections to some of the roots of a family tree.

Sometimes simple details can put items in context. Like the notes scrawled on the back of my grandfather's photos, valuable little pieces of information—time, place, and person—can help create a patchwork of detail that gives some structure to allow a family to reassemble the jigsaw pieces of a life. I'm grateful for the time my grandfather took to write down these little details. They help tether the images to real moments in time rather than leaving them more ambiguous.

Timecard is a device we built in our lab that uses these details left by my grandfather to reassemble a chronology of his life. It acts like a digital photo frame, showing images of my grandfather in a slideshow. Touching any image that appears on the device reveals a timeline that shows the other items from his suitcase. Timecard is intended to support storytelling about my grandfather by or for visitors. It is also a device that is designed to encourage reflection on his life. Seeing photos placed chronologically lets me understand the order in which events occurred, as well as watch him visibly change as he ages. (See Figure 5-2.)

Items on Timecard are added manually because the photos have to be scanned and the details written on the back typed in. Some of the burden of recording these details of a life is being lifted as such details become a routine part of the new things we create, as digital technology stamps facts into artifacts. Modern cameras can write the date and time, and increasingly the location, as a bundle of data that travels with an image, for example. The folders we create to store the photos away have names that provide more clues about the origin of their content. These facts about our digital things will provide priceless detail for contextualizing them in the future, not replacing the stories about them necessarily, but creating triggers for reminiscence. Just as seeing a face or item in a photo can aid in recall, so too can knowing when or where the image was taken.

It is not just the details embedded in a modern digital image that provide new forms of context that we didn't have in the past. Much of the data we create every day, from the mundane to the deeply personal, is stamped with a creation time. Emails, text messages, blog posts, and Facebook and Twitter status updates are all logged by time. All of this detail, brought together in time, can create a supporting context for a moment. By bringing together a message and an image, for example, created around the same point in time, a new sense can be had of what a person was doing then. Each item provides reinforcing detail that helps flesh out what took place at that moment. (Social media "scraping"—the gathering of such information by strangers—is also a significant topic for Internet security firms.)

Figure 5-2 Timecard, showing a timeline of my grandfather's life.

While all this content, stamped by time, can create connections that tell new stories about specific moments or periods, digitally reflecting on someone's life has its issues. A big issue is simply the volume of items we might inherit. Unlike my grandfather's few hundred photos, a digital legacy will likely soon include hundreds of thousands of items, created and kept over a lifetime. How are family members supposed to make sense of this, to pick out items of significance?

In the past our ancestors have implicitly indicated that an item is significant through the simple act of keeping it. Although thousands of objects likely crossed their path over their lifetime, the constraints of money and space meant that only a few were retained, often the most significant. With digital things, indicating significance is no longer a natural byproduct of us taking care of our items but instead becomes a chore. It takes effort to sort through virtual files and folders, and it's likely that instead this store of items will remain relatively messy and disorganized.

All of this implies a shift in the means through which we reflect on a person's life. Instead of having a limited number of significant items left by the deceased, and perhaps a few stories from them or from the people who knew them, we are likely to have far too many details of their life, the mundane mixed up with the exceptional. Rather than wishing we knew more about the deceased, we might feel that we now know too much.

Technology may provide some solution for this. Search engines such as Bing and Google do an incredible job pulling significant items from billions of webpages based on short search terms. The kind of ingenious thinking that makes this possible could be brought to bear on personal content; some breakthrough piece of software could do the work of extracting the significant from the everyday. This is not a trivial computer science problem, however.

Having the computer automate the process of making sense of a legacy is not just difficult but could be counter-productive. I created Timecard, described above, as a way to reflect on my grandfather's life. The process was a very manual one, eased by the fact that he left a limited number of photos behind. In that sense it was not unlike creating a photo album about him, with items carefully selected, descriptions added, and all ordered chronologically. It's possible that a piece of smart software designed to make sense of a vast store of digital content could have created Timecard for me automatically, but I'm concerned that automation undermines the act of reflection. I took time to craft the contents of Timecard, and that process gave me the chance to absorb more deeply the individual events represented in the body of photos I had at hand. I'm much more acutely aware of the contents of that device because of the act of creating the structure within it. I think this tension between the burden and benefit of making time to create new artifacts with the traces of a life is quite commonplace.

We might use this big digital legacy for reminiscing in other ways. We could end up having a relationship with the deceased through these items that is more abstract and serendipitous. Rather than trying to structure and corral all the digital pieces of a legacy, maybe we will choose to experience it randomly, like a vast digital photo frame that picks and displays disconnected photos from a large collection. Within this experience we might not know the stories behind all the content we see, but we will get a sense of the depth and breadth of the life of the person who passed away. That might give us a form of reflection that is based less on a deep understanding of the context behind the content. Instead the experience may seem more cinematic, and our role may be more as an audience than a storyteller.

Many of the messages and photos we create are quite mundane, but with the passing of time they can take on additional significance. Significance is a moving target. This is an issue I mentioned in Chapter 1, "Getting sentimental," when I described the lady who had inherited diaries from her mother and grandmother. To her, the mundane entries offered an insight into the lives of the deceased that she may not have had otherwise. The same is likely to be true of the tweets and other status updates we are posting online today. In the short term we might not see their value but in the long term they may offer a valuable resource not just for our reminiscing but also for telling the day-to-day story of our lives to our offspring.

Backup Box, shown in Figure 5-3, is an object that we've designed and built to encourage discussion around this issue. It is a simple wooden box containing a touchscreen that is connected to the Internet, constantly backing up a person's tweets. We imagine that it would be left doing this for years, accruing a history of activity over decades. The more it consumes, the more valuable it becomes as a record of the past.

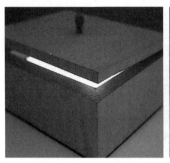

Figure 5-3 Backup box container and timeline of tweets.

At some point in a person's life, perhaps when they are older and thinking more about their past, they might sit down with this box, open the lid, and use the screen to scroll back through their life. Tweets, which seemed mundane when they were created, might now remind the viewer of the places, people, and events they cared about in their past.

On the owner's death, Backup Box might be passed on to another family member, its contents creating a valuable resource for reminiscing. Eventually Backup Box would be passed through several generations, and everyone who knew the person whose life is recorded in the box will have passed away. At this point its contents become archaeologically interesting, a sociological record of another time represented through the output of this life.

Backup Box is, of course, speculative. The irony with modern technology is that it doesn't have the level of robustness needed to last through successive generations. Backup Box's screen, for example, would barely last a decade let alone multiple ones. It is important to think hard about what it means to produce the fragile objects we do today, objects that are not robust enough for the scenario I just described. We may lose records of value as a result of such fragility.

One issue with all of this digital legacy is that it is likely to contain items that the deceased never intended anyone to see. As I've mentioned, physical items are filtered and kept within the constraints of the space available in our homes, but digital items take effort to discard. We know that deeply personal physical love letters, for example, found in a bequest were kept for a reason and are likely sentimentally significant. By keeping these items, a person is implicitly expecting that they will be found and read by others. With decades of email and other forms of digital communication, however, old messages might simply have been left in the archive of digital things, with no expectation of them being unearthed by others. The chance of coming across something unexpected that is decontextualized and upsetting seems higher. This is as true of online content potentially captured by a device like Backup Box as it is for offline content. Even though tweets and Facebook posts are made public by default, it's common to regret their posting in retrospect. Once an item is made public on the Internet, it is virtually impossible to take it away again. As we mature, the compromising things we posted online can come back to haunt us. Learning this is now part of growing up.

This gives the sense that the deceased do not control the way in which they are remembered, and that this is somehow a modern phenomenon. I suspect this has always been the case, though. A legacy is always under the control of those left behind. A process of filtering takes place once the deceased has passed away, as objects and stories are kept or discarded, shared or not shared. These choices can change the way in which an image of the deceased emerges and persists, not always for the better.

Grieving

Issues of death and grieving are extremely sensitive. Much of the focus on death as an issue within the technology industry has been on the impact of a bereavement online, where this sensitivity meets the harsh glare of billions of users. The rituals and norms of many cultures can meet and clash in this event, and the anonymity of being online can make people say and do things they might not otherwise. Sometimes this can be a good thing and sometimes less so.

Bereavement on a site such as Facebook is quite common now. With half a billion members it is bound to be. In many ways there is not a perfect answer for what to do with an online profile when its owner passes away. Initially, Facebook did nothing in the event of a death of one of their members. One issue that emerged, though, is that people who knew the deceased but who were not yet friends with the deceased (in a Facebook sense) started to see that person recommended as someone they should connect with, which was obviously upsetting. The deceased individual was still in the system, still treated the same as any other member of the site, and was still part of the processes of recommendation and friendship.

Facebook can now "memorialize" the profile of anyone on their site who friends or family prove has passed away. The profile becomes frozen and is no longer recommended for new connections. Existing friends of the deceased can still comment on posts, but no new friendships can be created. Existing friends can still express their sense of loss on the profile by adding their own comments to it, a practice that is quite common in the case of online bereavement. This process of expressing grief or loss online, in public, is an example of a practice that seems celebratory and positive to some and out of place and inappropriate to others.

Facebook's solution of memorialization means that any friends or family who were not connected with the deceased through Facebook are now locked out of this online process of grieving. It's common for parents to not be friends with their children on a site like this, yet once their child passes away they can feel a tremendous sense of support through the discovery of this sympathetic online community that has been left behind. Not being able to respond to this group because they are locked out from participating is a problem.

Ultimately, death is hard to design for. It is a change in state, a change in relationship with an individual, which is unpredictable and highly emotive. Of course the absolute solutions created with digital technology cannot properly address it. Even the application of technology to the traditional processes of bereavement seem somehow insensitive and out of place. Some funerals are now broadcast across the web, for example, using video-conferencing technology. This feels at once enabling, because remote friends and family can participate in a way they were not able to before, while also potentially having the effect of undermining a ritual that is usually sombre, sensitive and about physically being together.

This uncomfortable fit of technology and bereavement is not a new issue, as most things aren't. When the still camera started becoming more commonplace at the tail end of the 19th century, many people took advantage of this new technology to take photos of the recently deceased. Lacking the photos from a person's life, which we take for granted today, this opportunity to record the person after death was a final chance to create a lasting reminder. Families would prop the deceased up in a way that helped create the illusion of life, even posing in group portraits, the dead with the living. To us this practice seems quite macabre, and I suspect it also seemed a little odd over a hundred years ago, but in some ways it's easy to sympathize with this final attempt to preserve the image of a friend or family member, even in a way that maintained the illusion of life.

Honoring the dead

Part of the process of remembering someone is through the act of creation. Family and friends often put together photos and notes in a photo album or create a collage of images in the deceased's memory. This is a form of honoring the dead. Through these sorts of objects we celebrate a life, make it special, and in some way move towards preserving and persisting it. This process can be a collaborative one, with family members sharing what records they have of the deceased, as well as the stories they know.

This process happens digitally, too. A lot of the content that is a part of creating an artifact like a photo album is distributed and shared through email and the Internet. And many sites and services now exist that allow a family to create and print their own book of a life.

These objects don't have to take physical form. 1000Memories.com, for example, is a site that allows family and friends to come together and share photos, songs, video, and text to create memories of an individual. (See Figure 5-4.) It encourages the sharing of stories by showing prompts, such as "What is this person's favorite food/nickname/place?"

1000memories.com doesn't have a physical equivalent. It exists entirely online. I'm not sure whether it has a role as a long-term record of a life. I can't find any way to save it offline. My personal attitude towards many online services is that I don't assume that they will persist. I'm using very few of the services that I signed up for a decade ago. Our relationship to most services is fragile and fickle, and we move from one to another as they disappoint us, as something brighter and better comes along, or as our social group tempts us away. Perhaps it is just me, but I can't bring myself to make too huge an investment in any one service with the knowledge that one day I may just walk away from it. I want some sense of persistence in the digital structures I make in my life. This is also true of the structures I might make to honor someone who has passed away.

Figure 5-4 1000memories page for my grandfather.

Part of our goal in creating physical artifacts such as photo albums is to make space in our homes for the memory of those who have passed away. We want to keep a record and representation of them around us in order to avoid forgetting them. The Digital Slide Viewer, mentioned in Chapter 3, "Where the physical and the digital meet," was created to explore this relationship between the online services where many memories persist and our homes in which we want some sense of persistence of the deceased. It is a device that backs up an online account (in this case from Flickr.com) for posterity, in a form that is designed to persist and be kept with the other artifacts that we might have of someone who has passed away. Through objects like this we have the reassurance that the memories of the deceased are with us, that they can be shown and shared in the intimacy of our own homes. And as long as the online account persists, we have the advantage of all this content being able to be shared with family who are remote, too. That gives a sense of reassurance, even while it has less of a sense of permanence than the physical item that resides with us.

A continuity of relationship

There's a sense of obligation inherent in looking after the legacies we inherit. In most cases, of course, we want to keep these objects around us, and we want to make items in memory of someone who has passed away, but this sense of need is coupled with a sense of duty. It is our job to remember the family members who have gone, just as we would wish our family to remember us. It is our job to fulfill the wishes of those who have passed away, even if that can sometimes be a burden.

Sometimes the forms of remembering are ritualized, undertaken yearly on an anniversary associated with the deceased, for example. In Chinese culture the annual Qing Ming festival honors family and ancestors. During this period paper objects are burned in the belief that they will become real in the other world, which the deceased now inhabit. Genevieve Bell, an anthropologist working at Intel, has uncovered shops selling paper versions of everything that the deceased might need in their new state, including money, watches, lipstick and, increasingly, the digital things in our lives, including laptops and flat-panel televisions. Genevieve even talked to a family who burn a paper version of the newest mobile phone every year for their ancestors, in order that they may always have the latest thing. They thoughtfully include paper prepaid phone cards.

In our field work we have also found that there is a continuity of relationship with the deceased, despite their demise. Sometimes this is sustained technologically. One lady we spoke with kept a memory card on which were stored many personal text messages exchanged with her husband. She kept the card in a small wooden box, taking it out annually to reminisce with the contents. Another lady we talked with buried her husband with a mobile phone to be able to continue to text him and leave voice messages for him. These examples may sound strange when they are explained dryly like this, but perhaps they give these individuals an opportunity to say goodbye and let go at their own pace. Inevitably, these rituals are likely to be undertaken less and less by them, and perhaps managing this slowdown for themselves is a good thing.

Just as there can be a continuity of communication from the living to the deceased through objects, the reverse can also be true. A bequest, for example, sends us a message from the person who passed away that tells us what they thought of us, what they associated us with, and so on. Through the items left behind we can also find out more about the deceased and our relationship can continue to develop through this experience. Sometimes this is a positive thing and the artifacts that are left behind reinforce the relationship in a way that makes it more significant. Sometimes, though, the things we inherit don't fit into what we understood about that relationship and leave us confused and even upset, like the man I mentioned in Chapter 1 who inherited a box of rocks.

Letting go of the deceased's physical objects is difficult even if you have good reason. Whether you have no association with the objects, like the man and his box of rocks, or you have simply run out of space in your home, selling these items can seem a little mercenary. I've wondered whether services like Freecycle.org, which allow you to offer items for free to other people as long as they come and pick them up, might let individuals release themselves of the obligations of taking care of items they would rather not. Using Freecycle we can get a sense of these objects "going to a good home." We get some sense of the story and motives of the person who is willing to drive all the way to our house to pick up an item, and this can give us reassurance and alleviate our guilt about discarding the item.

This process of letting go is a subtle and difficult one, which digital technologies might exacerbate or alleviate. On the one hand technology can give us a form of release that is more gradual, that allows us, for example, to keep in touch with items remotely that we have had to let go of, so that we can forget them at our own pace. On the other hand technology might simply create experiences for us that never allow us to forget and move on but instead provide a constant reminder of the deceased.

In Part III, "New sentimental things," I'll talk about how new technologies offer ways of recording or reminiscing about our lives that can challenge or subtly improve the way in which we think about our legacy and the legacy of those who have passed away. These are new forms of digital heirlooms that may be both challenging and empowering.

Design challenges

There are a broad range of design challenges in this chapter that have to be approached in a sensitive way because of their emotive subject matter.

- → How do we design systems that allow us to formally include digital things as part of an estate on a par with more traditional artifacts?
- → How do we design experiences that allow families to deal with vast digital legacies?

→ How can we design digital systems that persist for the long term, both physically and digitally?

→ How do we design sensitive technological systems that enable broader participation in the act of bereavement and grief?

→ How can we design services for honoring the deceased that persist and feel owned by the participants?

PART III

New sentimental things

N PART I, "Stuff and sentimentality," I described my grandfather's heirlooms and I wondered how contemporary technological artifacts might change the experience of reminiscing. That led to some thoughts about the nature of physical things versus digital things. In Part II, "A digital life," I talked about some phases of life during which sentimentality about the past ebbs and flows in order to get a sense of when our history matters to us throughout our lifetimes.

Technology by its nature doesn't stand still, of course. The mundane digital practices of today—the pervasiveness of digital cameras or our use of social media, for example—were foreign to us a decade or so ago. In this part I want to speculate a little about the changing nature of technology and social practice to theorize a little about how radically different the digital things of our future might be and how they might impact the forms through which our reminiscing takes place.

I hope this won't be taken as an act of futurology. I'm nervous about predicting the future, particularly in the digital domain, in which big changes in the ways we record, arrange, and broadcast our lives are almost always unforeseen. Instead I'll try to pull together various ideas and projects that I'm aware of to paint a picture of a multitude of ways in which reminiscing might be changing as we age.

CHAPTER 6

Things and experiences

I n Chapter 4, "Our digital lifespan," in the discussion of phases of life, I mentioned how my wife and I had bought a DVD of ancient episodes of Sesame Street for our daughter. We were using modern technology to give her the experience of what we considered to be the best possible children's television, entirely biased by our own memories of childhood. In this chapter I'm interested in pushing further this idea that technology allows you to re-create experiences and situations for others. These are not the same as the original experiences, but the question is how they differ, and what value does an original artifact or experience have if it can be continually resurrected in new forms?

New ways of recording, duplicating, fabricating, and broadcasting can all create shifts in time, place, and material that allow us to question the value of "the original." Digital technology has already confused this issue, with a copy of a Microsoft Word document, for example, having as much value as the source file from which it was duplicated. The physical world might become similarly skewed as scanning and three-dimensional printing techniques develop, allowing for easy duplication of objects that are visually indistinct from an original.

With a loosening in the concept of "the original" because of the ease with which it can be re-created and re-experienced, perhaps we will be released from the anxiety of preservation? Why worry about taking care of an object if it can be regenerated at will? Instead, perhaps our legacy will take the form of pointers to digital records of the past, which can be re-created on a whim.

I'm going to explore this idea with an emphasis on ways in which we might re-experience places, things, and people.

Capturing places

Let's first take a look at how we can hold on to physical and digital places as we and our loved ones move through them.

Preserving physical spaces

When someone passes away, the person leaves the "baggage" of a lifetime behind. The executors of the estate, typically family members, have to make decisions about all of it. They have to deal with assets and liabilities, with virtual entities like bank accounts, and with physical artifacts like books and furniture. Often they also have to deal with homes, with the spaces that the person occupied, deciding whether they should be sold, and so on.

Unlike objects, though, which can be removed and preserved, these spaces have to be prepared for new lives, stripped of the memory of a previous inhabitant. Yet they can be just as sentimental and play as important a part in reflection on the past as any object. Just as the artifacts of a person's life can have sentimental associations for family members, so too can the spaces they occupy. It's common to remember ancestors in terms of the places they spent time. I remember the little shed that my grandfather spent a great deal of time in, for example, packed with tools, jars of nails, and other paraphernalia.

Microsoft has a technology called PhotoSynth that has made me think a little about what it might mean to preserve a space like this toolshed. PhotoSynth creates dynamic collages of two-dimensional photos that it arranges in a three-dimensional space. It can calculate not just when two photos overlap, but also the point from which each was taken.

Because of this, it overlaps them three-dimensionally rather than on a flat plane. Clicking each photo moves the viewer's perspective so that the viewer is perpendicular to it.

With this tool I could have taken a lot of overlapping photos of my grandfather's shed and, in essence, captured a version of it that I could then navigate around. By taking photos at both a distance as well as close up on the details of the tools, I could have created an experience of the shed that allowed me to "stand away" from it and see the context of it, as well as "peer closer" to see the small details of the space that my grandfather occupied. Figure 6-1 shows a PhotoSynth of a guitar workshop created by a member named "stringcraft." Viewers can start by looking at photos of the space from a distance through contextual shots and then zoom all the way into the three-dimensional space to look closely at guitars and tools in the detailed shots. This arrangement preserves a sense of the space and the details of the way it was used by its occupant.

Figure 6-1 A PhotoSynth created from photos of a guitar workshop. Left: A contextual shot. Right: A close-up.

New digital tools like this could help us preserve some experience of places that in the past we would have had to simply dismantle and forget. They could give us some sense of the relationship between objects within a room that could tell us more about how a former occupant used that space than a single photo could. Tools like PhotoSynth can create digital versions of a place that I would want to spend time in. The details of the space might nudge reminiscences that we might not otherwise have, and these digital spaces might form a new category of heirloom that documents a family's history in a compelling and useful way.

My grandfather's shed is long gone, unfortunately. In its place stands a newly constructed home. I recently returned to the village where he lived, and it was odd to have the sense of familiarity of the neighborhood, even while new lives occupied the spot where I once spent time. Geographically, the neighborhood has sentimental value to me even as it loses its familiarity. All places have this, of course, the sense of new history built on old. Technology, though, can offer ways of peering back through time, using place as a fixed element. For example, the website WhatWasThere.com allows people to overlay old images of places onto more recent ones. The site can show a shot from 1935 of an intersection in New York, overlaid on a contemporary shot taken from the same spot, for example. Figure 6-2 shows a mockup of the effect, using new and old photos of my old home. These kinds of experiences are made possible thanks to new mapping interfaces (such as Google Street View) that allow a virtual tourist to travel to another point in space to take a digital stroll through old neighborhoods. By overlaying old photos from the same perspective, we can take a stroll through time as well as space.

Figure 6-2 Overlaying old photos on new places.

Preserving virtual places

Digital technologies can help preserve physical space, allowing us to travel back in time, geographically, to places that we remember. What about the digital spaces that we now inhabit in parallel to the real world? Are the digital desktops where we spend so much of our time, for example, worth preserving in their own right, as structures that have value beyond the files and folders they contain?

In 2010, Emory University in Atlanta, Georgia, formally opened the Salmon Rushdie Archive. In addition to the notebooks and photographs you might expect to find as a record of a distinguished literary career, Rushdie also donated a desktop PC, three laptops, and an external hard drive, together containing forty thousand files and eighteen gigabytes of data. Rather than indexing all the content and putting all the files in one place as a reference, archivists at the university have instead re-created his digital desktop as he experienced it. Visitors can now navigate the content of these machines through the same interface that Rushdie used. The files on them are in the same places that they were when he worked on them, as are the applications, notes, and other detritus of the digital desktop.

There's a sense here that what can be experienced goes beyond simply the artifacts that were preserved. Instead, viewers can get a sense of the context within which they were authored and maybe gain an insight into how they came about in the first place. Emory University obviously thinks that the preservation of this experience of Rushdie's digital environment is important, just as the preservation of individual artifacts is. I wonder if this sort of preservation might also matter on a more domestic level, in addition to the academic one on which the University is focused. Now that we're starting to inherit PCs from our parents and grandparents as they pass away, is it interesting for us to preserve them as environments and experiences in their own right? There might be aspects of my father's PC, mentioned in Chapter 5—his choice of desktop wallpaper, for example, or the way he laid out his folders— that might remind me of him or tell me something about him that is unexpected. Perhaps I should see my father's hard drive as a place I could visit occasionally. Instead I see it currently as a big container of files, and I have this sense of obligation that one day they will all need sorting out. They are a burden when they should be a celebration.

Rushdie's old environments are emulated rather than experienced through the original hardware. Visitors to the archive don't type on the original keyboards that Rushdie used, but instead these records are hosted on a server somewhere that offers up different versions of the preserved systems, which run in a window on a modern computer. This allows the original device to be preserved in its own right, mitigating the risk of damage. It also allows multiple people to experience Rushdie's working environment at once. As Matt Buchanan from the technology website Gizmodo put it, "This is the power of what librarians and archivists call 'born-digital' material: it can go beyond preservation—bits are bits are bits, after all—and through emulation, you can actually inhabit his digital world, use the tools he used. You can't write in the leather-back books that Dickens did, but you can scribble in simulations of Rushdie's Mac Stickies. It's preserving more than material; it's preserving, in part, circumstance." Any changes that visitors make to that world can simply be reset back to a default state. That world can be preserved and any evidence of an audience simply wiped away.

The operating system of a PC tends to be a solitary place, managed by an individual and occasionally shared with a few others in a household or office. A lot of the digital worlds we are beginning to inhabit are social in nature, experienced by thousands or millions of individuals at once. Rather than being locked away locally in a laptop or PC, they exist online, distributed across the Internet. I'll talk more generally about our relationship to some of these online places or services in Chapter 8, "The things we put online," but I do want to mention here the preservation of some of these online worlds that have a strong geographical sense that isn't unlike a physical world.

I'm one of the millions of people who have played World of Warcraft, the hugely popular online role-playing experience created by the game developer Blizzard. I played for a number of months and wasn't drawn into it enough to be compelled to play every day for hours at a time as some are. Even with my lightweight experience of the game, however, with only a few hours grabbed here or there, I still have a very strong memory of the space I inhabited. I remember starting the game in a snowy, mountainous region, and I still have a sense of the crunch of the snow underfoot, the trails of footsteps left behind me, the gradual descent into greener places. These virtual worlds are fully realized in the sense that I have memories associated with places in them that I value. Figure 6-3 shows a character of mine riding a griffin, the equivalent of a taxi, in a shot I preserved, like a tourist photo, from the game.

Figure 6-3 Riding a mount in World of Warcraft.

World of Warcraft is a collection of fictional experiences that were hand-crafted for me by a team of people, who laid out every mountain and every tree themselves. It is a fabrication, yet my feelings towards it are similar in sentiment, if not strength, to what I feel about my grandfather's toolshed. And like that shed it will one day cease to exist, when the number of people who inhabit this world of bits dwindles and it is no longer economically viable. It will be another place that exists in the past, one that I wish I had some way to revisit. You could argue that this is not dissimilar to the worlds created in books and films, through radio and music, which can leave you with a pang of regret when they come to an end and a desire to return and re-experience them again. The freedom in a virtual world to get off the beaten track, though, to get out of the path of a linear narrative if you like, makes it feel different in nature and worth preserving in its own right. These are virtual geographies spread across real ones, hosted on servers around the world. They are not easy places to reassemble, and the videos posted online by their inhabitants might form the primary legacy we have of them once they are gone.

Capturing things

Physical places don't persist the way we remember them or might like them to persist. They adapt to new uses, new occupants. The best that can be done is for us to make recordings of these spaces to act as a bookmark in time and place. Because the original is not something that we can really preserve, the question becomes how we might best make a facsimile.

The same is not true of many of the things that make up our lives, the objects that we choose to keep in our homes. These are things we are able to choose to keep because they fit into the space we have around us. We keep lots of things, of course, for lots of reasons. Some are kept because of sentiment and some due to pragmatism. Some reasons are under our control, and some come about through a sense of obligation, because someone else makes a choice that we acquiesce to.

Capturing things to let them go

We will always have some of these objects in our lives, but do we really need all of them? How much could the capacity for digital technology to record these objects loosen our obligations to keep them as physical things? What is it that we are trying to do when we choose to persist these objects, and how much can digital technology fulfill these needs and release us from the necessity of preserving an original?

I've brought bits and pieces back home from my travels as a reminder of the places I have visited. Sometimes these objects are beautiful and

I want them to persist, like a glass bowl I brought home from Finland, which I have on display in my hallway. Sometimes these things that I pick up are quite kitschy and not really "me" at all, as a lot of tourist purchases are. I recently brought back a pair of bright orange plastic glasses with horizontal slits in them from a conference where I'd been given them for free. I really wish I hadn't. Yet they act as a reminder of an evening of fun. In this sense they don't play much more of a role in reminding me of my past than a snapshot taken on my phone or camera might. They are a reminder of a throwaway moment; the object itself is not precious to me. Taking a photo of these glasses and storing that image with the other photos of the conference would remove the need for me to keep the physical item itself.

Hector Serrano, a product designer in London, has taken this idea of digitally recording an object to preserve it a step further with his Backup Objects project. His idea is that we might capture our possessions as three-dimensional models, rather than simply flat images, as a new form of preservation. If we lose the original, we simply print it out using a 3D printer. This gives us the option to discard the original because we always have a backup of it in digital form. He has scanned a range of personal artifacts into the computer as a three-dimensional model and then printed them out using a 3D printer.

The three-dimensional capture process is rough because the technology is not mature. The same is true of the process of printing the item, which results in a duplicate that is not as high fidelity as the object from which it was created. The reproduction seems softer than the original, with a loss of detail. You could argue that this aspect of reproduction will go away as the technology improves. Digital photography was similarly low-fidelity when it first hit the market, but now the pixels of a modern camera are not discernible to the naked eye. I suspect that the reproduction can never replace the original, though. The qualities in material, weight, and finish, as well as the simple knowledge that it is a duplicate, will always mean it is self-consciously a facsimile. But for lots of objects, like my orange plastic glasses, this will be less of an issue because the artifact itself is not as precious as the memory of the event it is associated with.

Serrano thinks of these objects as a protection against loss, describing the project like this: "A series of objects with great emotional value for their owner that can be 'backed up' and then materialized by printing them with a 3D printer. Although the copy will never attain the same emotional value as the original, at least it can be a way of preserving the original in case it is lost, broken or stolen." He goes on to say, "As objects become digital we will be able to treat them the same way as word files, print, copy, download, or just send them on by email. How this will affect the way we produce, buy, use or share everyday objects?" This last point seems key to me. From the perspective of digital heirlooms, we might live in a world at some point in which we inherit not only the digital records we now expect—the photos, files, and other data—but also a record of our ancestors' possessions in digital form, reproducible at will.

There continues to be this question of why we like to keep a lot of the items we have in our possession. In addition to the twelve transistor radios I mentioned earlier that I bought in a frenzy of eBay purchasing (see Chapter 2, Figure 2-2), I also have a set of Star Wars figurines that remind me of my childhood but that I'm a little embarrassed to put on display. We now live in a world in which our physical collections of music, films, and books are becoming digital. These objects are no longer things that we put on display in our homes. Instead our tastes and preferences are represented in a way that is less tangible: as digital playlists shared online through services such as Spotify or Netflix, through our favorable or unfavorable comments posted as status updates in Facebook or Twitter, and through services such as Last.FM that track what we listen to on our digital devices and show us our preferences by using the real data of our listening habits.

I still have old, classic albums that I want to hold on to and keep in mind as a sentimental reminder of my past, as well as something I can listen to. As I transition my collection into this new intangible world, I've created playlists of "Favorite Albums" to keep track of them. I mark individual songs with "five stars" in iTunes in order that I might remember them. I try to maintain a connection with these items by using digital means. Through tagging the same is also possible for physical things. We can let go of them with less risk of forgetting them than in the past. I mentioned Tales of Things and BookCrossing in Chapter 3, "Where the physical and the digital meet," as two examples of services that allow digital properties to be attached to real items. The story of an artifact can be embedded or connected to the object itself so that as it changes hands some history travels with it and as it travels we can follow it and see new stories emerge. We can set our objects free into the wild through these services, safe in the knowledge that we keep some connection to them.

As we get used to living without a tangible expression of our media collections, without shelves of CDs and DVDs in our homes, for example, we might also feel less of a need for other physical things, too. Instead of feeling a need to own my transistor radios, for example, I may be satisfied with just expressing a preference for them online, showing that they're the kind of thing I like. Websites such as Things Organized Neatly and A Collection A Day, for example, provide carefully curated photos of beautiful but often mundane objects that are shared and celebrated through images alone. People take what they've seen on these sites and post them on their own websites, or to Facebook and Twitter, as a way of curating their likes and dislikes. In an article in the New York Times magazine entitled "Websites that collect stuff so that we don't have to," Rob Walker describes these sites as enabling us to enjoy physical things without owning them: "It is everything we love about stuff—but without the stuff. In a reversal of the desire to have your cake and eat it too, we can consume these lovely objects and not-have them, too."

Physical experiences of digital things

I'm not saying, of course, that we will end up living totally minimalist lives, devoid of objects, in which the deeply sentimental exists only in digital form. It is simply possible that our need to engage with physical things will lessen as our world continues to move beyond the screen.

It's also possible that the reverse might happen, that we might find that the shift of many aspects of our lives into digital makes us crave physical interactions more. Introducing a tangible element to the digital things in our lives may heighten our sense of them. The Playlist Player, shown in Figure 6-4, by Martin Skelly, for example, is a physical expression of digital audio playlists that plays on the nostalgia for the LP. Each "disk" is associated with a playlist of tracks and comes in a large sleeve. It mimics the ritual and social experience of the LP. I can imagine people sitting around this player passing around the album art as they listen to some new music, just as they did in the 1960s and 70s. This kind of experience is unlikely to replace the convenience of digital storage—it wouldn't scale to the 60 Gigabytes of digital music tracks that I own—but it might be a way for me to invest in and experience those tracks that are most precious to me in a way that is sympathetic, social, and almost ritualistic.

Figure 6-4 The Playlist Player by Martin Skelly.

Part of the sentimentality for LP records is in their imperfections, in the pops and clicks created by the small scratches and nicks on the disk. As I discussed in Chapter 2 ("Attributes of the physical and the digital") this sense of imperfection that comes from physical things is lacking in the digital because the digital doesn't age materially. The systems around digital things change, but the bits and bytes that make up the digital stay put.

This imperfection seems to be another element of physical objects that people crave. In the last few years there has been a growing adoption of photo applications such as Instagram—see Figure 6-5—and Hipstamatic that allow people to apply filters to their digital photos to make them look as if they were taken with old, analog cameras. This seems to be an attempt to make a mess of clean digital technologies. The most common filters applied to digital images mimic the kinds of photos that were produced by cheap plastic cameras that leaked light. It was the cheapness and poor construction of models like Lomo and Holga that created an aesthetic in its own right, one that implies spontaneity and uniqueness.

Figure 6-5 A digital photo with Instagram's "Lomo-fi" filter applied.

Now that digital camera technology is cheap enough to be almost disposable, we can start to play with devices themselves as a source of imperfection, rather than relying on software to mimic the experience post-hoc. I like this idea that we stop treating technology as fragile but instead see what qualities may come from it if we really mess with it. The Digital Harinezumi camera, available in Japan, takes this approach. It takes digital images and through a combination of software and hardware creates photos that are grainy and overexposed. It is a camera that seeks imperfection, something the manufacturers are very conscious of. They even plan to make the object you purchase unpredictable, by changing its qualities regularly. As they say on their website, "We intend to tweak the image quality with every new lot, every month. Some will even have an entirely different lens. This is our plan, to bring even more views, more uniqueness to each of these cameras."

It is hard to know whether there is a real craving for the experience of imperfection in the use of the software and hardware I've described, or whether this is simply another passing fashion sweeping across the Internet. Time will tell. I do get the sense that with so many digital cameras in the world, built into phones as well as dedicated units, it is simply difficult to feel that photos we take are interesting and unique. Imperfection helps give some experience of unpredictability, and therefore uniqueness, to the act of recording our lives.

Capturing people

Hopefully I've given you some sense of what it might mean to preserve or even re-create the *experiences* of the places and things in our lives. I wanted to touch finally on people as another subject that could be re-experienced through digital technology. When people pass away we are left with a few records of their lives that allow us to re-experience them through our senses. We have pictures of them, sometimes video, and in rare cases audio recordings that let us hear what they sounded like when alive. In addition to allowing us to reminisce about them, these records all provide ways in which we can pass some experience of them on to others, so that our offspring, for example, can get a sense of them without having ever met them in person.

Microsoft Kinect is a device not unlike a webcam that can also see in three dimensions, recognize a face, and understand the physical nature of the way people move. Through Kinect, people can engage with technology using their whole bodies. The system understands when they are waving, can see when they lift a leg, understands which way a person is looking, and so on. Through technologies like this we can start to imagine what it might mean to not just preserve images of people but also their shape and motion.

Kinect is at the forefront of a wave of accessible technology that allows us to not just see but also record aspects of individuals that might form a new way of experiencing them later. An extreme example of what this kind of technology is capable of was seen recently in the second Tron movie. Using three-dimensional capture equipment the team working on the film was able to create a digital version of the actor Jeff Bridges as he appeared when he was a 25-year-old. This digital body is decoupled from any specific activity. In essence it is a puppet. The motion of someone living, like the real Jeff Bridges, can be used as data to give it life, or the computer could put it in motion in other ways.

Perhaps what all this technology offers is quite mundane. It may simply mean that when we reminisce about our relatives we no longer have to do it through a two-dimensional image. Our records of them might allow us to simply see them from different angles as well as in motion. (See Figure 6-6.)

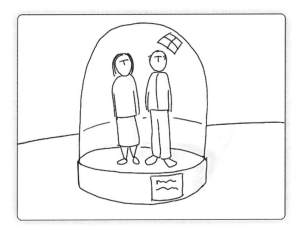

Figure 6-6 A three-dimensional view of my relatives.

Technologies like three-dimensional and motion capture could offer us a new avenue for the creation of our own legacy. To some extent they create a new form of digital immortality that is different from the still image and that might prove irresistible to many because of the way it offers to bring someone back to "life" after the person has passed away.

With a recording of someone in three dimensions, there could be new ways of re-experiencing the person that are uncannily real. It is probably too early to tell whether these are experiences we would actually want to have.

Much of this chapter has explored ways through which new technology might help us preserve the places, things and even people we care about in order that we have a record of them through which we could reminisce in the future. The activities I've described are not focused on ourselves but instead emphasize the role that we might play as archivists of the things around us that matter. In the next chapter I'd like to focus on our own lives, to explore new approaches through which we might turn the camera lens on ourselves.

Design challenges

Design challenges for this chapter focus on making sense of new ways of capturing people, places, and things.

→ How might we record people for posterity, other than through photographs and video?

→ How might we design systems that explicitly allow for the capture of places for reminiscing?

→ How can we design tools that allow participants in virtual places to create a record of their experiences?

→ How might we design digital systems that represent physical things in the richest way possible?

→ How do we design digital objects that have some of the more compelling aspects of physical things?

CHAPTER 7

Recording our lives

For hundreds of years people have taken on the responsibility for creating a record of their own lives through diaries, photo albums, and other artifacts. Even the simple notes on the back of my grandfather's printed photos (shown earlier in Figure 1-1) are an example of this investment in recording the personal details of a life. People like my grandfather might do this for their own needs, as a way for them to jog their memory in the task of recall when the time comes to reflect on the past. They might also create these forms of record with a view towards their legacy, as a way for their family and friends to learn about them once they have passed away.

Just as technology is creating new mechanisms through which we record the things around us (and not us), it is also providing new ways for us to record details of our own lives. In this chapter I will look at some new ways to think about the preservation of our lives.

Logging our lives

One of the more thought-provoking pieces of technology to have come out of the Microsoft Research Cambridge lab in the last 10 years is a device called SenseCam. SenseCam is a small, oblong digital camera that is worn around the neck on a short strap. Unlike a regular digital camera, which is manually triggered to take photos, SenseCam takes pictures automatically, once every minute. It passively chronicles a person's life, creating a record of both the mundane and the more interesting things that happen every day. (See Figure 7-1.)

SenseCam has a wide-angle lens, which catches a lot of peripheral detail in a shot. When hung around the neck it also sits not far below the wearer's eye line. It therefore produces pictures with a lot of contextual information in them because they come almost from the perspective of our eyes. The images it produces have an aesthetic quality that is quite distinct from the way we see, however, and the rich contextual information means that when these images are used to reminisce, they often bring new, formerly unnoticed details to the attention of the wearer.

SenseCam is recording constantly and produces hundreds of photos a day. It is able to do this because battery life and storage size are now large and cheap enough that devices like it are commercially possible. In the past it would have been difficult to imagine an object of its size being always on, constantly taking and storing away pictures. It's not just its portability that's interesting, though. SenseCam is an example of a new class of device or service that allows us to catch and keep the minutiae of our lives in an automated way. In Chapter 5, "A digital death," I mentioned the issue of nonmaterial legacies, such as our Twitter streams, that might be preserved for posterity through devices like the Backup Box (shown in Figure 5-3). Automated systems like SenseCam are an extension of that idea. They are another form of digital output from our lives, triggered without our intervention, which might be interesting for us to use in the future as a way of reminiscing about our past.

This idea of "life-logging" has been taken to its logical conclusion by Microsoft Research's Gordon Bell, who digitizes as many aspects of his life as he can into a system he calls "My Life Bits". This includes shots taken with the SenseCam, as well as "everything he has accumulated, written, photographed, presented, and owns (e.g. CDs)".

Figure 7-1 The SenseCam device and a sample shot taken while on a bicycle.

Many devices and services that record our lives for us automatically are already in common use now. They, too, can be set up to observe us over prolonged periods of time, recording what we do, where we spend our time, who we see, and so on. Last.FM, which I mentioned in the previous chapter, is a music website that allows you to track the songs you listen to (an act it terms as "scrobbling"), drawing on the data about your listening habits provided by many different devices and services. I joined this service in August 2004, and since then the site has logged 13,390 times I've listened to a song. These are not songs that I've listened to through the Last.FM site itself (or at least very few are). This data comes from the Windows Media Player software I use on my PC, the iPod I listen to on my drive into work, and even the home audio system through which I listen to songs in my home. All of these systems send play information to the Last.FM site.

This data collection was enabled by me at some point but has long since become a background process that I rarely think about. It is now a form of data utility, like the electrical supply, flowing from my home rather than into it, a part of the plumbing of my life. Occasionally I go to the Last.FM website and through this data I can reflect a little on my listening habits. I can see which artist I've listened to the most (The Ting Tings), or which songs ("Take a Chance," by the Magic Numbers).

This data provides a snapshot of me that, like my Twitter stream, may be far more interesting as a source of reminiscing about my life than it is now. It's not that interesting to find out what I was listening to last week, or even last year, but finding my favorite, forgotten bands from years ago is much more compelling because of the way it allows me to reflect and reengage with my past.

The Nike+ system similarly logs my behavior. Rather than tracking my use of media, it records my footsteps. The system consists of a sensor that is worn in a running shoe and a second receiver that can be attached to an Apple iPod or worn around the wrist like a watch. The sensor tracks the jogger, detecting the swing of their foot over the duration of the run, and calculating how many steps and what distance they have covered. All sorts of details of the run can be calculated from the raw data provided by the sensor—the distance, the average pace, the time of day—and then uploaded to a website run by Nike and shared with others.

This idea of tracking data and statistics about oneself is known formally as Personal Informatics. As with many ideas, it is not a new one. People have kept track of their weight using scales for years, and we've had fun in our home tracking the growth of our daughter against a wall chart, as many parents do. We've had to remind ourselves to do these activities, though. What technology enables is for this to be a continuous, passive activity in which we don't have to remember to record any statistics; we just have to remember to look at them occasionally.

This shifts the point of self-reflection. If I had a system that continuously monitored my daughter's height, for example, I'd lose out on the excitement and celebration that comes about when we gather around her to measure her manually. We lose the act of recording as an event. We might need to find other means to celebrate the achievements recorded through these devices. Perhaps we might look at the data on my daughter's height at her birthday, instead, making it an annual point of reflection, celebrating a year of growth.

Not all of these data gathering devices need to be automatic, of course. We might develop devices designed to specifically capture data about our lives for explicitly sentimental reasons. Kjen Wilkens's Weather Camera—see Figure 7-2—is a working but conceptual device that captures the wind speed, temperature, and other attributes of a place, rather than a digital image. Kjen imagines that this data about a place could be used for recall, just as imagery of that place could, and that this nonvisual information might have its own form of sentimentality.

Figure 7-2 The Weather Camera by Kjen Wilkens.

Nicholas Felton is a designer who has taken this notion of personal informatics to its extreme (or you might say to its logical conclusion). He celebrates the data of his life each year by publishing his annual Feltron Report, an example of which is shown in Figure 7-3. This is a summary of his year in statistics. He started in 2005, with his first report describing in pictures, charts, and numbers how he spent his time. One page describes his year in music, with details such as the number of songs he has played in iTunes (16,862). Another describes his eating habits. A small pie chart shows how 28% of the restaurants he visits make Sushi and 24% focus on "Domestic" dishes.

Figure 7-3 A page from the 2007 issue of the Feltron Report.

The first report from 2005 feels most like a pastiche on the corporate report in the way it is designed. Its cover is a very industrial-looking shot of machines harvesting grain. I suspect it started a little tongue in cheek. With subsequent issues, though, the process seems to have become more personal and thematic. In his 2009 report he drew on data from his friends and family to provide a picture of his social network and his place in it. His 2010 report is based on the life of his father, drawing on artifacts and information that he left behind when he passed away. What started out as a seemingly facetious commentary on corporate reports has developed into a thought-provoking annual publication with interesting insights into how Felton spends his life, and it is now extended into his familial and social networks.

As Felton demonstrates, this data, seemingly cold and slightly clinical in its raw form, can create a narrative of sorts for our lives that allow us and our family to reflect not just on single numerical instances— representing where we've been, what we've done and who we've seen for example—but also over time to consider how we have changed. Annual reviews of this kind of content are likely too regular for most of us. There is only so much navel gazing a person can handle. As a source for reflecting on decades or a lifetime lived, however, data like this might provide an invaluable, complementary resource to go along with the photos and artifacts that are a more typical part of a legacy.

It is possible that some specific data points about us might become emblematic of us and elevated above others. Just as the runs batted in (RBI) in baseball is symbolic of a batter's skill, so too there might be certain numbers in our lives that we hold up above all others. In the Xbox Live online service, which allows computer game players to compete with one another, a player's Gamerscore represents perseverance with the system and, to some extent, skill in it. It is a value that accumulates with play, and players with a really high Gamerscore like to show off their stats by embedding this score visibly in their blogs, on Facebook, and so on. It is a badge of honor for them.

A more physical example of this elevation of data is shown in Figure 7-4, with a project called the Encoder Ring. As described by the project's creators, "Encoder Rings began as an investigation in how to store precious or personal digital information. The result is a series of rings that are decorated with tiny blobs and holes that actually represent letters in binary code; the code used as the basis for digital information." I like the subtlety of this project. The dots and blobs look simply like a decorative pattern, but for those who recognize this arrangement for what it is, this artifact can represent much more.

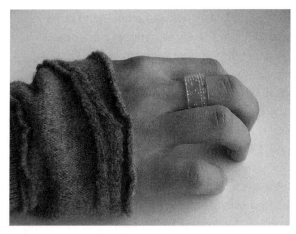

Figure 7-4 The Encoder Ring.

It's not hard to imagine many other examples of data from our lives that we might print out, wear, or put on display to celebrate different aspects of our achievements. These would then act as heirlooms that represent the things that mattered to us. Like the digital avatar from World of Warcraft, printed out and made physical—see Figure 3-9—to provide a real instantiation of a virtual world, perhaps there is value in making some of these significant statistics of our lives into real things. I might choose to print out a little data trophy representing my first 500 miles run with the Nike+ system, for example, as a way for me to celebrate and share this achievement.

Playing on the senses

I've talked about the potential of not just digital artifacts like photos to serve as a valuable part of our legacy but also data in a more raw form, which can create an alternate record of our lives. Let's shift back to more physical sources of potentially sentimental content but stay away from the visual items that have dominated the discussion so far. We tend to think of visual media and artifacts when it comes to legacy, but digital technology could change our relationship with the rest of our senses, too, just as it has with the visual, providing new ways of recording and recalling the things we hear, smell, and touch.

We know that the sounds we hear as well as the smells and tastes we pick up around us can be tremendously evocative in terms of recall. Smell, particularly, can transport us to moments in our past in a way that is tremendously visceral and instant. I smelled cut grass last week and was immediately transported in my head to Welton, a village in the North of England, where I spent many summers as a child. I didn't have to seek out the memory in the way I might have to with a picture. It came instantly. It wasn't even a specific moment in time that the smell connected me to; it was the sensation of a place not an event, one that I know from subsequent visits no longer exists. The French author Proust, famously, had a similar experience with taste, transported to his childhood by a bite into a Madeleine, a French pastry. He coined the term "involuntary memory" to describe this effortless form of recall.

It is surprising that, with all of this power as an aid for recall, the senses of hearing, smell, and touch (and even taste) haven't been developed more in technological terms. Perhaps that is an indication that there are nontrivial issues for each.

Audio

In terms of the things we record and keep, audio plays a supporting role to the visual senses primarily through video. Video without audio seems archaic. It's a silent movie. But with audio the visual just seems to become stronger, even if all you hear is music and not dialog. The audio reinforces the visual. It can do the same with still images, although there is not really a great model for combining these two forms of media— visual and auditory—in a way that makes them complimentary and easy to experience. David Frohlich, Director of the Digital World Research Centre at the University of Surrey, suggests a solution this, an object he describes as an AudioPhoto, an idea he presents as one example of how digital technology may transform the way we record and re-experience our world.

There is power in recording audio alone, of course, without visual content, since it allows recall to take place in our heads. By listening to audio without video, we can let our heads create a picture of places, events, and people that isn't bounded by the frame of the camera.

But audio is slippery as a medium within which sentiment might be embedded. The question of context, the boundaries within which audio is operating, is one issue. Audio can be in the foreground of an event. Hearing someone speak, for example, or listening to music from our past can help in the recall of a person, place, or event. Sometimes it is the background noise of a place that is evocative, that gives us a sense of activity and ritual. Hearing the clatter of utensils in a family kitchen or the sound of a crowd in a stadium can be very evocative. Background sounds by their very nature, though, are not things we notice at the time. It is common to be oblivious to the hum of air-conditioning in an office, for example, until it is switched off because our minds filter it out. A lot of sounds in our homes and lives are like that.

It's hard to take a snapshot of meaningful audio, in the way we do through the camera for our visual senses, because of this issue of background and foreground. We ran a study into the use of digital audio for recall with various families in the region around our Cambridge laboratory. We gave each family a digital audio recorder and asked them to go around their homes and record the sounds that were meaningful to them. Later, we had them listen back to what they had recorded.

We found that for many family members it wasn't the subject of the recording that was meaningful to them—it was what they could hear in the background, what they had accidentally recorded, that was most evocative. It was only through the act of recording that they stumbled across sounds that were meaningful. In our report on the work we wrote "We refer to these sounds as sonic gems, so called because, although they were precious, these sounds were often previously unconsidered, buried alongside or under other soundscape elements, and uncovered only through the recording and playback exercises." This experience of recording audio would be like not knowing if a picture, taken with a digital camera, was of an important moment until after it had been taken and viewed.

I'm not sure what a solution might be for this issue. It makes audio recording an ephemeral thing because pinpointing what's meaningful about the sounds around us is difficult. As highlighted by SenseCam, technology has reached a point where battery life and digital storage space offer amazing new experiences. In the case of audio we now have hard drives that are large enough that they could allow us to record and keep every conversation we have in our lifetime, if we chose to. Much of it would be noise, though, with a few sonic gems buried within. Part of the issue here is around tools for listening. I can fairly quickly browse a hundred digital photos to pull out my favorites, but tools do not exist that allow me to do the same with sixty minutes of audio. This area of sentimental audio seems quite unexplored.

The visual form of audio—the sound wave—has become quite iconic. The idea that you can represent sound visually is quite a powerful one.

A wave representing sound is mysterious because it's basically a code for the ears, one that requires a machine to provide a translation. In the Waveform Necklace project by David Bizer (shown in Figure 7-5), visual representations of sound files are printed out as bracelets intended to act as tokens of love or as a mysterious representation of some meaningful audio. Like the Encoder Ring shown in Figure 7-4, it is easy to imagine elevating these sound snippets for their own sake, as aesthetic artifacts with hidden meaning.

Figure 7-5 The Waveform Necklace by David Bizer.

Some other senses

If the sense of hearing seems unexplored as a medium for sentiment, the sense of smell is even more so. Instinctively, there is something vaguely ridiculous about the idea of recording a smell, let alone "playing" it back to reminisce later. Yet we know that smell is very powerful in terms of recall. As a sensory organ the nose has a more direct connection to the limbic system within the brain than other senses, which implies it may have a more direct effect on emotion and long-term memory. However, unlike our visual and auditory systems, which are at least quite well understood, we don't have a good understanding of what goes on when we smell something. We know that odor molecules enter our nose and they fit into particular odor receptors designed to recognize them, like a key fits into a lock, and this fires a nerve cell. Beyond that, it's a mystery. We don't know how the molecule is recognized in the first place, for example.

Technologically, there are tools that allow for the capture and, to some extent, recognition of odor. "Electronic noses" are used industrially to tell if food has gone bad. These are still quite primitive. The re-creation of a smell is even further behind technologically and can bring to mind the scratch-and-sniff card craze of the 1980s. In 2000 a company called DigitScents announced a USB peripheral for the personal computer, called the iSmell, which contained a cartridge of 128 odors that could be released in different combinations in response to commands from the PC. They imagined, for example, that a certain smell might be released when a particular website was visited. The company folded in 2001 before the peripheral was released.

Smell likely has all the complex issues described earlier with sound. Identifying and isolating the "olfactory gems," the ones that are really meaningful, would probably be equally problematic, if not more so. Even if we could capture the smells we wished to keep for posterity, the process of re-experiencing them would likely be problematic. Smells cannot be targeted and contained the way that visual or auditory data can. And there seems such a fine line between a pleasant smell and a potentially noxious one.

Still, the notion of bottling up the smells of cut grass in the summer or of bacon sizzling on the grill (two of my favorites) seems compelling. Who knows what technological breakthrough might make this more practical?

I won't go into the potential for taste as another channel for digitally recording and reproducing our senses to connect us with our past. To some extent the problems of capturing and re-creating taste are similar to, and bound up with, smell. Suffice it to say that just as there is an "electronic nose," there is also such a thing as an "electronic tongue."

Finally, while smell and taste have a way of connecting us with a sense of our past, it is not clear that touch does. I don't have much of a sense of the feel of objects I held and played with as a child. Plastic feels like plastic, after all. We do associate age with materiality, though. We describe objects as aging gracefully, with some materials doing this better than others. Leather softens with use, and wood acquires a patina through the nicks and scratches it picks up or the layers of varnish it receives. A lot of these properties have a strong sense of haptics to them—a need to actively explore them through touch. We often can't resist the urge to touch things that have aged.

As I've mentioned, objects are changed through touch. Tools that are used over extended periods of time change shape as they adapt to continual use, and in this way become more tied to their owners, like the handles of hammers which become smooth as they're held the same way for year after year. Perhaps touch is a sense, then, that plays a primary role in adding to the history of our things, rather than helping us recall them later.

Our sense of touch could play a role in providing another channel to help bridge the digital with the physical. The Phantom force feedback system from Sensable, for example, was developed to give us a sense of touching a virtual object. Devices such as this are intended primarily for product design, giving people a tool not unlike a mouse to virtually model new objects on the screen and "feel" the object they are creating while they do it. We could imagine them playing a role with our sentimental things, too, particularly those we might archive through a system like the Family Archive, described in Chapter 3, "Where the Physical and the Digital Meet." (See Figure 3-10.) In this way we could not only see objects we'd preserved digitally from our past but also virtually hold them in our hands.

A spontaneous relationship to the past

What is clear from this chapter is that digital technology brings with it a myriad of new ways in which we might record and recall aspects of our past. Devices like the SenseCam and Nike+ already allow us to continually record our lives and reflect on them in new ways, taking the established activities of photography or diary keeping and, to some extent, automating them. Other devices and systems will emerge that do something similar in new and unexpected ways.

All of this points to an explosion in content about us. The legacy of sentimental content I will leave to my daughter will not be as straight-forward as my grandfather's was to me. There will be a lot more stuff, and a greater variety of it. I was able to browse through my grandfather's photos in two short sessions. My daughter probably won't have the time or the inclination to do the same with all that I leave, and I can hardly blame her—she will inherit the 200,000 digital photos I anticipate taking manually in my lifetime and all of these other things I've created as a side-effect of living.

Without the time to reflect on this content in any methodical way, it's likely her experience of it will become more haphazard. She may dip in and out of the things I leave behind at random, experiencing it in a way that is less structured and far more spontaneous and serendipitous. I'm not sure this will be such a bad thing. This might give her a different experience of reflecting on my life than is traditional, but it will not nec-essarily be a less meaningful one.

New systems could be built that explore more diverse ways of experiencing digital legacies beyond simply going through everything methodically. These systems might play with notions of time, for example. There are a large number of blogs and Twitter streams that already publish diaries from the past in digital form, playing with time by posting entries on the days of the year on which the originals were written. I can currently read the diaries of Orwell, Thoreau and Pepys through public blogs that publish entries exactly 67, 152, and 343 years, respectively, after they were originally authored. This is true for less significant figures, too. On a more personal scale the grandson of William Henry Bonser Lamin, an "ordinary soldier" in the First World War, published his grandfather's letters from the trenches exactly 90 years after they were originally written. The final entry, posted to the blog on January 12th 2010, corresponded to the last letter he wrote after his discharge on the same day in 1920. By posting on the same day the reader gets a sense of the regularity and rhythm over which the original items where created, as well as a sense of the seasons.

Imagine this kind of experience for personal rather than public consumption of sentimental, bequeathed content. A system like this might pull items daily from a vast digital legacy, making certain things more significant because they occurred on the same day, displaying them in the home and providing a recurrent way of reflecting on someone else's life.

Time is not the only significant property that might trigger the display of content from a digital legacy. Geography is another significant attribute. Just as the idea above pulls items out of the digital store because of the similarity in time, a similar system could be developed that pulls from this store of digital content because it was recorded near the same place that the viewer currently stands. It might be evocative for my daughter to stand on the banks of the Thames at some point in the future and find out that I'd jogged past their regularly when she was a little girl. This experience is a more personal version of the place-shifting ideas described in Chapter 6, "Things vs. experience," and shown on sites like WhatWasThere.com (see Figure 6-2).

Connections through time and space may provide compelling ways to pull from a vast digital store, but in the end randomness might be the most straightforward approach. We may simply rely on systems that pluck a varied set of items from this store and hope they both help give a general sense of a life lived while also revealing new and unexpected things about a person to us.

The digital photo box shown in Figure 7-6 is a prototype built by Mark Selby, while he was at Microsoft Research Cambridge, that explores this idea. It is a wooden box with a closed lid that contains a small photo printer. At unspecified intervals the device selects one item randomly from a store of digital photos, printing it as a physical photo. The delight in the device is in not knowing what you might get when you open the lid. Once a photo is printed you can choose to archive it away in the box itself, or put it on display in a small frame. Gradually a picture emerges of the life that the images represent as more and more are printed.

Interestingly, sometimes the mere fact that a photo has been selected and physically printed seems to make it more important somehow, regardless of what the subject of the image is. The fact that it was picked makes it matter as does the fact that it was "promoted" from digital to physical form.

Figure 7-6 The digital photo box.

Although I've talked a lot about what our digital legacies might be formed from, and to some extent how we might experience them, so far I haven't explored the new places in which they are being kept. Our physical estates have tended to be domestic, with sentimental things kept at home with us, on display around us, or in the boxes we store in our basements. Digital things can be kept on the PCs and laptops in our offices and bedrooms, but increasingly they actually live more ambiguous lives outside of our homes, on the online services we use every day. We keep our photos on sites like Flickr.com and our messages in

Facebook. They live on servers that might be in the same country as us, but are more likely to be overseas somewhere. In Chapter 8, "The things we put online," I want to explore our relationship to these services and talk a little bit about how they are changing the ways in which we might contain our digital legacies.

Design challenges

We need to design new experiences that make sense of the data of our lives.

→ What forms of data might our lives produce, and how might we present and emphasize them in ways that allow us to celebrate and reflect on what we achieve?

→ What new experiences might we design for recording and reviewing audio that might make it more easily browsable, tangible, and useful for reflection?

→ If we could record and recall people, places, and things through all of our senses, not just sight and sound, how would we represent them and experience them through our digital systems?

CHAPTER 8

The things we put online

I n earlier chapters I mentioned a variety of online sites and services through which new digital legacies are being created every day. On Flickr people share photographs, building up a record of the places they visit, events they participate in, and people they meet, which are likely to form an interesting archive for the future. I've talked about the mundane, diary-like nature of the content we broadcast through sites like Twitter and Facebook and the value it might have in the long term for reminiscing.

These sites have become such a way of life for many people that it is hard to remember that only relatively recently did the Internet become a place where we put things. Initially the web was a resource primarily for finding out about things. Creating a webpage was something that required an esoteric knowledge of HTML, as well as a server to actually host the content. It was only through the popularization of blogs and other tools, which simplified the act of publishing, that it became more commonplace to share content with others. We need to treat the Internet as a new frontier that forms a part of our digital legacy. The things we create as an offshoot of our lives don't just live with us, in our homes; they live in new forms in a virtual world, which extends well beyond our immediate surroundings.

Since I've been considering the topic of digital heirlooms, I've become conscious that whenever I post something online I may be leaving behind a small piece of my history, another breadcrumb in the story of my life. As Rob Walker put it in his New York Times article, "Cyberspace When You're Dead," "Sites and services warehouse our musical and visual creations, personal data, shared opinions and taste declarations in the form of reviews and lists and ratings, even virtual scrapbook pages. [...] We pile up digital possessions and expressions, and we tend to leave them piled up, like virtual hoarders." Rob is making the online world sound not unlike our homes, filled with stuff that is messy, that builds up, and that perhaps we lose track of.

In this chapter I want to focus on our use of the Internet and the challenges and opportunities it brings to issues of legacy. Online storage offers both great reward and great risk with issues of heredity. It offers reward because of the rich strata of information it can preserve. It enables new forms of legacy that are quite unlike things we would have inherited in the past, which will offer new insights into our ancestor's lives. It creates risk because of the fragility and disjointedness of our day to day online world. I'm not simply talking about administrative issues, such as the way in which we pass on our website passwords when we die, which I discussed in Chapter 5, "A digital death." More broadly I'm talking about the casual way in which we think of the Internet as a series of places that we have only a temporary engagement with and how little we worry about persistence of content within them. I'll talk first about issues that emerge with online content that are challenges for the accumulation of personal legacy. Afterwards I'll draw attention to a few new services and trends that indicate alternative ways in which we might think about our online estate.

Things live all over the place

I mentioned Flickr, Twitter, and Facebook as places where I keep some of my digital things. These are not the only sites I create content in. I haven't mentioned many of the other services I use on a regular basis, like my two blogs (one that mixes my work and personal life and one that I use to track new and interesting technology trends), Delicious.com (where I store bookmarks to websites I want to remember), Evernote.com (where I copy web content that I want to preserve for another day), eBay.com (where I buy and sell physical items that are a part of my live), and so on. Each has its own purpose in my life, fulfilling some need. Each has its own password and profile. Each has content that I've created that is unique to it. And all of these sites are dispersed, disconnected from one another. Each exists as its own entity, devoid of much connection with the other sites I use, and this is problematic when it comes to understanding the extents of a digital estate.

When my father died I had no way of knowing what sites he might have invested time in, which might contain content that he had authored. I was pretty sure that I had a good sense of the extent of his physical possessions, which were defined primarily by the four walls of his home. I even had a good sense of the extent of the digital things in his life that he didn't put online, because I knew they were likely on the hard drive of his computer (shown in Figure 5-1 in Chapter 5). But his online life was and still is a mystery to me because of the lack of a real record and connection between the virtual places where he spent time.

Our investment in our online places isn't likely to diminish. Far from it. "Cloud computing," a term and set of ideas that have grown in prominence over the last few years, encompasses a set of services and technologies that will push our lives even further online. The Internet will become not merely a place for storing and sharing our digital things but a technology resource in and of itself. Instead of thinking of the Internet as a place we publish content to, it will become the place within which we undertake the activities that we might have done on our personal computers in the past.

I'm currently writing this book on my laptop in my home office. The document that I'm editing lives on the hard drive that is physically encased in this device. The version of Microsoft Word that I'm using to author it is installed on the same drive, represented by a set of files and settings distributed in various folders. In five years' time it is entirely possible that this picture will have changed radically, that both the file I'm editing and the tool I'm using to edit it with will be online instead. Even today, an online version of Microsoft Word exists, hosted on a website rather than on my laptop. In the next few years it may become a dominant way to author.

The advantage of storing my document online and using a hosted tool is that I'm not restricted to a specific device for editing. Instead, I can do my work using whatever device is conveniently at hand. I might do "serous" editing of it using my laptop at home, connected to the online version of Microsoft Word. I might then review and tweak the same manuscript, this time using my phone, during my daily commute. Again I would be connected to both the files and tools I need through the network.

This is quite a different working environment than the one represented by Salman Rushdie's laptop, in which there is a trace of the person in their devices that makes the devices themselves worth preserving. (See the section on "Preserving virtual places" in Chapter 6, "Things and experiences"). Mr. Rushdie's laptops are brimming with the tools and files he used to do his work, and the arrangements he created within the devices are interesting because of this. In a world where both our files and tools live online, our relationship with our devices becomes even more transient because of the lack of real content on them. We will use these devices primarily to work on items that are distributed across many different sites and services; we can swap these devices out pretty easily because preserving what they contain is less of an issue.

From the perspective of legacy this change may be positive. Rather than inheriting multiple devices, each with its own set of files and tools, we could instead inherit digital files that are distributed, but hopefully not duplicated, online. Less duplication may mean that there is less sorting out to do of the content once someone passes away. But the issue remains of how we find out about the location of this distributed content in the first place.

Not places for life

This issue of the distribution of content is exacerbated by the transient nature of the sites we use. One of the great things about the Internet is the casual way in which I am able to try out new sites and services with little commitment. Most services are free at first, and many are "free for life," so it is always tempting to create a new profile for myself on some new site that I've been recommended just to see what it might allow me to do. Yet as I sporadically try out these different sites I leave behind me a trail of personal, possibly sentimental content that is easily forgotten and lost.

I can try these sites on for size, if you like, to see which ones actually persist and are added to the set that I use for the long term. For each of the sites that I've actually settled on I've often tried a number of others that offer similar functionality. Before I settled on Flickr.com as a place to share my photos, I had tried Google's Picasa service and more traditional photo-printing sites like Kodak.com. Flickr fit my needs because the people there tend to be photo enthusiasts, and I'm keen to improve my skills as a photographer.

I'm constantly tempted away from Flickr to try something new, though. I've played with Instagram, for example, which focuses on quickly sharing photos taken on a camera phone that look digitally aged, and I'm currently tempted by Color, an application that again runs on a phone and would allow me to share photos with people in my immediate surroundings.

I do have some sense of loyalty towards Flickr partly because I think the service is very well designed and partially because my investment in it since I joined in 2005 has resulted in a body of over 1,500 images, all shared, tagged, and organized into sets with similar themes. I understand that switching to another service would be a painful experience, but I'd probably move somewhere else for the right set of reasons. In the end, all of the photos I've posted on the service live somewhere on my hard drive.

While I played around with Instagram I posted a number of images to their site, including a few of my daughter. I have a few more images posted up on Twitpic.com, a service that you can use for sharing images when publishing to Twitter. I may never use either of these services again, yet they have both got content on them that is a part of my personal history.

Just as there is a short-term attitude towards the hardware we own—an expectation that we will replace our phones every eighteen months, for example—we also have a short-term attitude to the sites that form a part of our lives. I can imagine and certainly hope that in twenty years or more I'll still have my old analog photos that are in a box in my store room. I can also imagine that over the same timeframe I'll still have the digital photos I've kept at home, albeit on a different device to the one I'm using now. I can't imagine at that point, though, that I will still be using Flickr. I expect something new and shiny to come along and draw me away.

I am sure there were many people who were extremely invested in MySpace.com. At its height (2007 to 2008) the social networking service consistently beat out its main rival, Facebook, in attracting the most visitors to the site. Participants in the site spent time constructing and maintaining their personal webpages, just as they do on Facebook. Yet by 2010 their customers were leaving in droves, many to their rival. Their number of unique visitors plunged from 96 million to 63 million visitors during that year. There might be all sorts of reasons for this decline, of course. Facebook may have pulled customers over by offering a set of tools that were more compelling. MySpace may have pushed customers out, too, by creating an environment that was cluttered and dominated by advertising.

Online services need to persist in a form that is useful to me, but instead they constantly change as they navigate their demands for growth. It is not just my own fickleness and lack of loyalty that may make me leave Flickr. Flickr may push me out as the business decisions that they make become incompatible with my wishes for the site. I exert some tiny influence over Flickr through the way in which I use the service, but they are a business, of course, and need to be seen to evolve to meet their requirements for income and their need to stay relevant. I think that Flickr, specifically, has done an amazing job meeting the needs of its customers. The seven years I have persisted with, and invested in, the site is a testament to this. Seven years is a lifetime online. Who knows, though, how the winds of change (which blow at gale-force in the online world) will drive them in the future.

Ivor Tossel described the ultimate result of our fickleness with websites best in his article "On the Web, forever has a due date":

> Picture yourself sitting in front of your news-o-scope (my patent is pending) when up pops word that a website you were really into a decade ago is shutting down. "Facebook!" you exclaim. "I remember Facebook! I posted 250,000 pictures to Facebook. My lost youth!" If it sounds improbable that everything you've piled into Facebook might evaporate in just 10 years, then consider: One of the biggest websites of the late 1990s is about to get deleted. At the end of October, Yahoo will pull the plug on GeoCities, the service that more than 1 million people used to set up web pages. On Oct. 27, the whole thing will simply cease to exist. It will, as we say in the industry, go poof.

Changing notions of the public and private

Our lives online, then, are both distributed and transient, issues that are problematic when it comes to the preservation of legacy. Both of these make it hard to get a sense of the estate of an individual since their "belongings" are scattered here and there and piecemeal because of a lack of time spent in any one place. But it's not just the place-ness of the things we post online that affects the way we might think of them sentimentally. They are created, to a great extent, as public by default, and this changes the nature of them as a record of a life compared to items that are private and personal. We publish on the Internet primarily to share with others. We do this with an audience of friends or family in mind, but our content is also often read by strangers. This is quite different from diaries and other personal content that we find as part of a physical legacy.

Diaries, particularly, are written as personal, private records of a life. There is a sense that they might ultimately be read by some other individuals, but the emphasis in their creation is on observation and honesty, on providing an outlet for discreet thoughts that reveal what a person actually thinks but is unable or unwilling to say publicly. Online content, by contrast, is written with a sense of audience, in a way that helps the author project a certain version of his or her being. This isn't necessarily deceitful, and it doesn't make the things they post less valuable as a record of a life, but it does make them a little different from things that weren't created publicly because of the choices the author may have made for what to include and omit, what to emphasize and what to play down. Online content needs to be filtered through a lens that gives a sense of what the writer's goals were.

In addition to this sense of audience, posting content online also raises questions about privacy and ownership. Online services can be quite protective of their rights to any content posted on their systems, and there is a sense of ambiguity in the question of ownership. I'm not entirely sure, for example, that I "own" the photos that I post to Flickr or, at least, what rights I gave away when I put them online. What rights does Flickr have to distribute what I've shared through their site to third parties, without my knowledge?

Services are generally resistant to portability of content, too, discouraging ways of backing up or moving items out of their domain. It is in their interests to invest in features that keep their customers rather than ones that might tempt them away. This attitude does raise problems when it comes to the preservation of content for the long term. In the online world, tools and content are tightly bound. On my laptop they live separately.

Online content is somehow both fragile and persistent. As I've discussed earlier, it has fragility because of our relationship to the services on which personal items are stored. Online content is also persistent, though, because items that are posted online can end up being both publically and privately duplicated. Publically, as items are referenced, remixed, and rebroadcast by others. Privately, as our personal data enters the mysterious, hidden pathways that allows it to move from one company's database to another.

All of these serious and sensitive issues surrounding the way we share our content can undermine the value of it all as a record of a lifetime because it tends to put an emphasis on short-term control. We want to share, but we are not so sure that we want to be remembered, since our musings can last and can be open to misinterpretation if they are re-presented in a context that we didn't intend. This pushes countries like France, for example, to explore laws that would require online services to delete users' content after an agreed period of time or simply when they demand. It's easy to sympathize with the need for these kinds of approaches as a solution to online issues of public and private perception, but I can't help wondering what sentimental content might be lost as a side effect.

Looking forward

Online content offers up some issues, then, when it comes to legacy because of the nature of services and the sense of the Internet being a public rather than private place. For the rest of this chapter I want to focus on some approaches to the online world that might help mitigate these issues or offer alternative ways of thinking about our estate in the cloud.

I'm going to describe four different strategies for preserving our online content so that we can maintain some sense of it and preserve it as a resource for our families and friends. I don't think any one of these strategies is necessarily the dominant one. As with many aspects of our lives, online individuals are likely to create some cocktail of any or all of them if legacy preservation is something they want to address.

The four approaches involve

→ Backing up our content somewhere as we create it.

→ Connecting the disparate places where we keep things.

→ Moving our content from place to place.

→ Creating one central place where our content always lives.

Backing up

In 2010 the Library of Congress announced that it was going to start backing up Twitter, creating an archive for posterity of the millions of public updates posted on the service. Many significant events have been recorded, been celebrated, or even taken root on Twitter, and the Library clearly felt this made the site historically significant and a resource that should be preserved for study. As they said in their announcement, "Just a few examples of important tweets in the past few years include the first-ever tweet from Twitter co-founder Jack, President Obama's tweet about winning the 2008 election, and a set of two tweets from a photojournalist who was arrested in Egypt and then freed because of a series of events set into motion by his use of Twitter."

Part of the emphasis of the Library of Congress announcement was one of legacy. They were making the point that the Internet is a place that we should not only live in but also be able to look back on, that with the rapid pace of technological change there is a risk of losing histori-cally interesting material that we may regret not having access to in the future. Their interests are centered on history as a cultural resource, and they work at a national or global level, yet even though this book is focused on a more intimate, personal level, those same issues of persis-tence are true. How might our content be archived and preserved, too, lest we forget?

There are some services that try and preserve and present a snapshot of our online past for us. The Wayback Machine, for example, regularly trawls through online sites, taking and preserving snapshots of them, in a way that is quite agnostic about the source. Since 1996 it has preserved the state of millions of websites. Type the address of one of them into the Wayback Machine and it presents a list of all the snapshots it has available for that site. You can use the site, for example, to see what Microsoft.com looked like when the Wayback Machine first kicked into life in the year 1996.

As the Internet has grown, the Wayback Machine has struggled to keep up with the billions of websites published online. It doesn't store images since they would take up vast amounts of hard disk space, so the snapshots that are presented to you are mostly text and structure, with broken image links. The snapshot of a site that is image heavy can look very bare because of this. It is not just images that the system struggles with. The Wayback Machine was also created in an era when static web pages coded in HTML were the norm, but many modern sites don't work that way. Instead they are created for you on the fly from a database of content and personal information. Without knowledge or access to that data, those sites don't make sense.

A personal approach has to be taken, then, if we are to rely on backing up as a strategy to preserve our online content. The responsibility has to be ours because no service is large enough to contain the entire Internet. In addition to working at a personal level, any system we use for backing up has to have a sense of the data from which our online experiences are created, otherwise much of what we get may have structure but won't have the content that is meaningful to us.

Backupify, for example, describes itself as a site that "backs up all your data on services like Twitter, Facebook, Gmail, Flickr, WordPress, Blogger, and YouTube. The service keeps all the raw data for you and creates a downloadable PDF with, for instance, all your Tweets, direct messages, followers, people you follow, and profile info." It is great that the service catches not just personal detail but some of the context, such as social relationships, that can be so rich for reminiscing. It is interesting, however, that the option of creating a PDF is offered here. There is something comforting about offering the content in a form that has a sense of persistence. The Backup Box device, which I described earlier in Chapter 5 (see Figure 5-3), plays on this same sense of fragility and the knowledge that content simply feels safer in our homes rather than online.

Backupify and services like it are attempting to create some sense of reassurance in the fragile relationship between us and the sites we use by offering to preserve content from those sites. In the end, though, the Catch-22 of Backupify is that it is itself a service and has all the same fragility associated with it. It may change in ways we don't like. It may cease to exist if it fails to become a viable business. We might need a backup for our backup.

Making connections between places

I mentioned earlier in the chapter that one issue with our online sentimental content is that we scatter it across the internet as we use different sites and services. One strategy I've mentioned is to back it all up into one place. Perhaps another strategy for addressing this issue is to have a system that attempts to tie together and help us keep track of these disparate locations. We would keep things where they are but use this system as a catalog of our content.

There are already many solutions for systems that help keep these connections in our memory. We can simply maintain a list of our most invaluable websites by bookmarking them through a web browser. We can even share these bookmarks publicly, through sites like Delicious. com. We can create a more curated version of this list and offer it as an online public face to represent key elements in our digital estate to others. Sites such as AboutMe.com, for example, provide an online "business card" that acts as a gateway to all the significant content and services connected to an individual.

Some sites use this list making as part of the process of bequeathing. Legacy Locker is described as a service that "lets people store details for every online account they use, from Gmail and Facebook to eBay and PayPal. They can assign different digital assets to different beneficiaries, who are entrusted with access details in the event of the customer's death or disability. Users can also prepare letters for the loved ones to whom they've entrusted their accounts."

LifeEnsured.com not only helps maintain a list of sites that matter to a person but also allows them to have actions performed on those sites in the event of their death: "Besides having Facebook accounts deleted, users can leave a final status message, disable wall postings, change their bio (theoretically to the past tense) and even transfer ownership of the account. In fact, LifeEnsured members can take similar actions with over 30 online services like Twitter, PayPal, WordPress and Dropbox."

The issue with the systems I've described here is that they are manual. They require an explicit act on the part of an individual to list the places that matter to them. Because our relationships with these services are fickle, it seems unlikely that many people will remember to update these lists as new services become important to them and old services diminish.

The degree of importance of any individual service matters, but it is constantly in flux. Sites like AboutMe.com tend to put the emphasis on sharing just the significant things in our lives, since those are the things that we would want others to see. There is risk with this emphasis, both that the less significant may be lost and that the significant may slowly become less important. Saying that, one positive attribute of AboutMe. com is that it offers practical value in giving us an overview of our online life that makes it easy to access the tools we use every day, as well as share our online domain with others. It offers value to the living as well as to those who are thinking about their legacy.

It is possible that our online accounts and profiles could play a role in tying together our disparate sites. An account on Windows Live, for example, can already be used across a broad range of services offered by Microsoft, including those that deal with managing email, gaming profiles (through Xbox), and devices (a Windows Live identity is used on the Windows Phone). So this identity ties together a number of services that matter to me.

There are a large number of these profiles, though, and the question is whether any of these individual identity systems might become a standard and come to encompass a majority of the sites I use, rather than being limited to those offered by a specific company. It is becoming quite common in the UK and US, for example, for new sites and services to use a customer's Facebook profile for logging in and account management rather than use their own proprietary system. With that profile comes all the social data that the new service can take advantage of straight away. What this means is that my profile becomes something through which disparate sites are drawn together. An identity system like this becomes convenient shorthand for me and the things I care about online.

Content mobility

A third strategy for helping preserve our online content is to make it simpler for us to move it from one location to another as we shift from service to service so that we become less likely to leave behind things on a site that we may forget we ever used. Personally, I quite like this approach. I don't like the idea of having multiple sites that do, generally speaking, the same thing. I like focusing on one tool at a time that has a certain purpose. I like to stick with Flickr as my photo-sharing site, for example, and would rather avoid starting to share pictures through another site because of the fragmentation and duplication that might cause. I like the idea that when I chose to move from one photo-sharing site to another, I can simply take my content, and all the investment that it represents, with me.

There are services that purport to help enable this mobility. Cloudkick. com announced a feature called CloudShift that "lets customers transfer data between different cloud-computing providers with just a few clicks. It makes it possible to shift an application from Amazon's servers to those of competitors, such as Rackspace, with surprising ease. This means that businesses using Cloudkick can avoid being locked into one provider—a feature that could help save money if a different provider suddenly offers a cheaper service."

The emphasis in this quote is on business systems rather than personal use, though, and I've found little evidence that CloudShift is a reality beyond the source company's original announcement in 2009. And, as I mentioned earlier in this chapter, service providers tend not to encourage portability of content anyway since it puts an emphasis on their customer's departure.

The way that the tool (the service) is so wrapped up with content is quite different than the offline world of applications and files, which are quite distinct. In the online space my data is all bound up in proprietary systems that struggle to exchange content, so that even if it was a feature that was offered regularly, content portability wouldn't be straightforward since it requires compatibility between the system from which the content is drawn and the system to which the content is being moved. Many of these systems now consist of data rather than static webpages, so the databases of both systems have to have the same concepts and containers for different pieces of information. It can be easy for things to break.

Centralizing our estate

A final strategy for helping with the preservation of our online content is centralizing the place where our content is stored. Rather than distribute our data across the Internet, we might imagine that it always lives in one place, a place that belongs to us. The different services we use might draw on that place and add new content to it, but the source itself would be our property. In this sense it would be similar to the offline world where the tools I use are kept separate from my data. When it comes to legacy, my offspring would only have to worry about one centralized place.

There is plenty of naivety in this approach because of the way content is distributed online and the way that services come about, but to me this feels most like the way I live my physical life—the things that belong to me are kept in a place that is also mine. It also feels like the least explored from a service perspective. Perhaps that is because there's no such thing as "my" place on the Internet; I'm always going to rely on a service to provide me with storage space of my own, just as I do with my blog. Perhaps it is also a chicken-and-egg situation that comes about through a lack of infrastructure. A system like this doesn't exist now, so where is a new service supposed to get all this content from and save new content to?

I do consider my blog, though, to be the only slice of the Internet that I really have control over, even if I pay someone else for the space where I keep it. Part of the reason I consider my blog to be mine is that it is a decentralized system rather than a centralized effort like Twitter or Facebook. I carefully selected the host that would make space for my blog, and then the host enabled the tools I would need to customize and post to my blog. The place came first and then the choice of tools I wanted to use. With modern services, these tend to be tightly bound together. You can't use a service without the place also being set for you.

So, the tools and content are tightly bound. I can't look at the posts I've created online without using the system that created them. The pages on my blog are not like the document I'm editing right now, which exists as an element in its own right. In reality my posts exist in a database somewhere, broken into pieces, looking nothing like the original. The question is what is really mine in these new systems. How can I trust that what I create in them is of lasting value, preserved as a record of my life, even if the tools that I originally used to author them cease to exist?

Design challenges

I've presented four strategies for dealing with our online legacy in this chapter. Each has its own advantages and disadvantages, challenges and opportunities.

→ How can we design systems for backing up and preserving our content online that don't in and of themselves feel as fragile as the services which they persist?

→ How can we design systems that help us more easily keep track of the sites that we care about and also give us some sense of what we have invested in each?

→ How can we design systems that encourage content mobility as well as make content between services mesh comfortably?

→ How might we design a set of services that all draw from and write to a place online that truly belongs to me?

Afterword

In this book I've tried to describe the ways in which digital technologies may change the nature of legacy and make us rethink our attitudes towards the sentimental. It's clear that a number of large shifts are happening in the way we see our personal estates. As physical things become digital, and as we start to leave records of ourselves as a byproduct of daily life, the way we reminisce, and the way we will be remembered, will change. I suspect that in the next decade and beyond, the shadow of the Cloud will hover over all of this, as we start to take our connectedness for granted and as everything we do and see is recorded and published, if not shared, online.

A few years ago it felt to me that we were at an inflection point with our relationship with our online worlds that was centered on trust. Did we trust the Internet as a place where we might keep our things? The virtual world is a place of risk, open to misinterpretation, fragile, and changing. It is a place within which we may say too much about ourselves and find out more about others than we might wish. It seems at this point, though, that our commitment to it is inexorable. It has become something that we cannot do without.

I try to imagine what it would have been like for my grandfather to have lived his life in the connected way in which we do now. I wonder what I might have found out about him online that was unexpected. I wonder about the physical things I inherited from him and how many would have been digital instead if he had lived the life that I am living. Of course, it is impossible to put his lifetime in our context. The past is a different place, as is the future. Just as my grandfather's legacy is very different from the one I will leave behind, I'm sure my legacy will be quite different from my daughter's. The digital age is going to continue to change the ways in which we are remembered just as much as it is changing the ways we live.

References

Some of these references are going to seem a little obvious, since they are to sites and services that you may know well. Part of the problem with writing about legacy, though, is making reference to things that may be forgotten in the future. I feel the need to assume that the things that seem obvious now will be foreign at some point soon.

Chapter 1

The "box of rocks" and the "forty years of diaries" are described in "Passing on and putting to rest: "Understanding bereavement in the context of interactive technologies" (2010), by Will Odom and others.

The "adopted child's belongings," the "charred plastic gear," and the "inherited ladle" are described in "On human remains: Value and practice in the home archiving of cherished objects"(2010), by David Kirk and Abigail Sellen.

To read more about showing photos in our home "because we know we should," see "Photo displays in the home" (2008), by Laurel Swan and Alex Taylor.

Chapter 2

For more on "precious Microsoft Word documents" and "deeply personal email," read "On human remains: Value and practice in the home archiving of cherished objects" (2010), by David Kirk and Abigail Sellen.

"Microsoft Surface," an interactive, digital table: *www.microsoft.com/surface*.

Cathy Marshall describes four challenges for archiving our digital things in "Rethinking Personal Digital Archiving, Part 1" (D-Lib Magazine, March/April 2008).

"Macromedia Director" is a multimedia authoring tool now owned by Adobe: *www.adobe.com/products/director*.

"Adobe PageMaker" was a desktop publishing tool superseded by Adobe InDesign: *www.adobe.com/products/pagemaker*.

"Flickr" is a photo sharing website: *www.flickr.com*.

"Sinclair Spectrum 48k" was a personal computer that proved very popular in the UK during the Eighties. Not so popular elsewhere. See *www.sinclairzx.com*. For your entire Spectrum emulation needs, see *www.worldofspectrum.org/ emulators.html*.

Chapter 3

The iPod containing "music for Christmas" was observed in research done by New Experience Ltd. for Microsoft Research Ltd. (2010).

Mobile phones as "containers for intimate text messages" are one of the many subtle forms of communication discussed in Richard Harper's *Texture: Human Expression in the Age of Communications Overload* (MIT Press, 2010).

The "Digital Slide Viewer" was originally conceived by Mark Selby. See *www.richardbanks.com/?p=2172* for more details.

"Tales of Things" is a system for connecting objects to stories: *www.talesofthings.com*.

"BookCrossing" lets you release books into the wild and track them online: *www.bookcrossing.com*.

More about the "@1000TimesYes" paper archive of Twitter music reviews at *www.articlemethod.com/ART002.HTML*.

"FigurePrints" will 3D print your Xbox Live Avatars now, too: *www.figureprints.com*.

There is a video of the "Family Archive" system up on *www.richardbanks.com/?p=1947*.

Chapter 4

Abigail Sellen and Steve Whittaker talk about "the 5 Rs of memory" in "Beyond total capture: A constructive critique of Lifelogging" (2010).

The "three key recipients" of sentimental objects are described in "On human remains: Value and practice in the home archiving of cherished objects" (2010), by David Kirk and Abigail Sellen.

Taking photos as a "form of celebration" of an event is described in Richard Harpers's *Texture: Human Expression in the Age of Communications Overload* (MIT Press, 2010).

"eBay" is an online auction site: *www.ebay.com*.

"Sesame Street" is a popular American children's television show: *www.sesamestreet.org*.

"The virtual possessions of teenagers" is discussed in "Teenagers and their Virtual Possessions: Design Opportunities and Issues" (2011), by William Odom and others.

The Long Playing ("LP") record and the Compact Disk ("CD") are material forms of music storage that have been, or are being, superseded by digital alternatives.

"The Reminiscence Bump" is described in "Things learned in early adulthood are remembered best" (1998), by D. C. Rubin and others.

"Rosy Retrospection," like the "Reminiscence Bump," is one of a number of cognitive biases that impair judgment: *en.wikipedia.org/wiki/List_of_cognitive_biases*.

The "Amazon Kindle" is a device for reading electronic books: *www.amazon.com/kindle*. Their system for lending digital books is described at *www.amazon.com/manageyourkindle*.

Chapter 5

The "Wells Fargo digital vault" is described at *www.wellsfargo.com/wfonline/wellsfargovsafe*.

For more on "Timecard" and "Backup Box," see *www.richardbanks.com/?p=2172*.

"Facebook" is a social networking site for sharing thoughts with friends: *www.facebook.com*. Their form for reporting a deceased person's profile, which starts the process of "memorialization," is at *www.facebook.com/help/contact.php?show_form=deceased*.

"Twitter" is a micro-blogging site for sharing short bits of text with others: *www.twitter.com*.

"Bing" and "Google Search" are systems for searching the internet from Microsoft and Google, respectively: *www.bing.com* and *www.google.com*.

Examples of Victorian "photos of the recently deceased" are shown at *cogitz.com/2009/08/28/memento-mori-victorian-death-photos*.

Genevieve Bell describes "Qing Ming" paper funerary technologies in an article written for Icon Magazine in October 2008, available at *www.iconeye.com/index.php?option=com_content&view=article&catid=420&id=3750*.

The "personal text messages" are described in "Passing on and putting to rest: Understanding bereavement in the context of interactive technologies" (2010), by Will Odom and others.

"Microsoft Word," a popular digital writing tool: *www.microsoft.com/office*.

You can view the "Guitar Workshop" at *www.photosynth.net*. Search for the words *Guitar Workshop*. David LaVallee created this PhotoSynth.

"Google Street View" shows street level images of buildings through a map interface. More details at *maps.google.com/help/maps/streetview*.

You can read about the "Salmon Rushdie Archive" at Emory University's site: *www.emory.edu/emory_magazine/2010/winter/authors.html*.

Matt Buchanan's article about "Rushdie's Mac Stickies" is titled "Walking in Salman Rushdie's Digital Footsteps" (2010) and is available at *gizmodo.com/5494443/walking-in-salman-rushdies-digital-footsteps*.

"World of Warcraft" is an online role-playing game played by thousands of people at once, published by Blizzard: *www.worldofwarcraft.com*.

You can read about Hector Serrano's "Backup Objects" at *www.hectorserrano.com/index.php?id=41&m=lab&grupo=backup*.

"Star Wars" is a science fiction world, with associated films and merchandise, created by George Lucas: *www.starwars.com*.

"Spotify" is an online music streaming service: *www.spotify.com*.

"NetFlix" is a video service that mails video disks to your home and also allows you to stream videos over the internet: *www.netflix.com*.

"Last.FM" is an online music service that tracks your listening habits and allows you to play "radio stations" based on your tastes: *www.lastfm.com*.

"Things Organized Neatly" is a collection of photos of different artifacts arranged in a tidy way: *thingsorganizedneatly.tumblr.com*.

"A Collection a Day" was a project by Lisa Congdon undertaken in 2010 in which she took photos or painted pictures of her own collections of objects. The output from the project has been published as a book (2011). Details of both are at *collectionaday.com*.

"Websites that collect stuff so that we don't have to," by Rob Walker, is on the New York Times Magazine website at *www.nytimes.com/2011/02/13/magazine/13FOB-consumed-t.html* and is part of Rob's excellent, and now ended, column entitled "Consumed."

You can find out more about Martin Skelly's "Playlist Player" on his website at *www.martinskelly.co.uk*.

"Instagram" is a photo-sharing app and service that is (currently) only available for the Apple iPhone. Details at *instagram.com*.

"Hipstamatic" is a photo-taking tool, available on the Apple iPhone. More information at *hipstamaticapp.com*.

The "Lomo" and "Holga" are classic film cameras famous for their cheap construction, which results in a distorted image that can be quite beautiful. Available at *www.lomography.com*.

More details about the "Digital Harinezumi" camera at *www.superheadz.com/digitalharinezumi*.

More about the "Microsoft Kinect," a camera that can see and interpret the human figure in motion, are at *www.xbox.com/kinect*.

Details about the digitization of Jeff Bridges for the movie Tron 2 at *www.guardian.co.uk/film/filmblog/2010/dec/06/jeff-bridges-tron-legacy*.

Chapter 7

You can read more about the "SenseCam," a wearable, passive camera, at *http://research.microsoft.com/sensecam*. You can even buy one at *www.viconrevue.com*.

"Gorden Bell's" webpage is at *research.microsoft.com/en-us/um/people/gbell/*, where there are also some details about his book *Total Recall: How the E-Memory Revolution Will Change Everything* (Dutton, 2009).

The "Windows Media Player" software for playing digital music comes with most, if not all, versions of Microsoft Windows.

Apple's iPod is a fairly common portable device for playing digital music: *www.apple.com/ipod*.

"The Ting Tings" and "The Magic Numbers"—nothing dates a person more than their taste in music.

The "Nike+" system tracks running performance and is available at *www.nike.com/nikeplus*.

"Kjen Wilken's Weather Camera" captures a snapshot of weather conditions and is documented on his website at *www.kjenwilkens.com/projects/sensor-poetics*.

Nicholas Felton's "Feltron Reports," tracking and presenting his life through data, are available at *www.feltron.com*.

The "Xbox Live Gamerscore" is accumulated by completing different "achievements" in Xbox games and is a general part of the Microsoft Xbox gaming platform: *www.xbox.com*.

The "Encoder Ring", which translates binary into jewelry, was designed by Jonathan Ben-Tovim and is detailed on the website PSFK: *www.psfk.com/2008/09/encoder-ring-binary-code-jewelery.html*.

"Proust" described the experience with the madeleine in his novel *In Search of Lost Time* (AKA *Remembrance of Things Past*).

"AudioPhotos," which combine sound and vision, are described in David Frohlich's *Audiophotography: Bringing Photos to Life with Sounds* (Springer, 2004).

"Sonic Gems" are described in more detail in the paper "Sonic Gems: Exploring the potential of audio recording as a form of sentimental memory capture" (2008), by Gerald Oleksik and Lorna Brown.

The "Waveform Necklace" was conceived by David Bizer. Details at *http://bza.biz/project/wavefrom-necklace/*.

The "Orwell, Thoreau and Pepys" blogs are at *orwelldiaries.wordpress.com*, *blogthoreau.blogspot.com*, and *www.pepysdiary.com*, respectively. William Lamin's blog is at *wwar1.blogspot.com*.

The Digital Photo Box is documented up on Mark Selby's website: *markmakedo.co.uk/excavating-digital-archives/photo-box/*.

Chapter 8

The article "Cyberspace When You're Dead" (2011) is available on the New York Times Magazine website: *www.nytimes.com/2011/01/09/magazine/09Immortality-t.html*. Rob also co-created *significantobjects.com*.

"My two blogs" are at *www.richardbanks.com* and *www.richardbanks.com/trends*.

"Cloud Computing," like "Web 2.0," which predated it, is an amorphous set of concepts and technologies and will mean different things to different people. Details of what Microsoft offers in this space are at *www.microsoft.com/cloud*.

"Google's Picasa" photo-editing software and service is available at *www.google.com/picasa*.

Kodak Gallery, a photo sharing and photo printing site, is at *www.kodakgallery.com*.

"Color", an app for sharing photos with those around you (available at *www.color.com*), is already starting to suffer from something of a backlash: *techcrunch.com/2011/03/24/color*.

The numbers highlighting the decline of "MySpace" come from Comscore via *techcrunch.com/2011/03/23/amazingly-myspaces-decline-is-accelerating*.

"Ivor Tossell's" article "On the Web, forever has a due date" (2009), was published on the Toronto Globe and Mail's website at *www.theglobeandmail.com/news/ technology/on-the-web-forever-brhas-a-due-date/article1310077*.

For more details about "France" exploring file deletion as a legal issue, see *news.bbc.co.uk/2/hi/programmes/click_online/8447742.stm*.

The "Library of Congress" announced the Twitter archive on their blog at *blogs.loc.gov/loc/2010/04/how-tweet-it-is-library-acquires-entire-twitter-archive*.

You can get to The Wayback Machine, which provides an archive of many websites, at *www.archive.org*.

The "PDF," or Portable Document Format, file was created by Adobe Systems and does a good job of completely capturing the elements of a document in a way that is very fixed and has a feeling of permanence about it: *www.adobe.com/pdf*.

"CloudKick" has gone mysteriously silent about their "CloudShift" service, for transferring data between online data warehouses, since first announcing it at Under the Radar in 2009: *www.undertheradarblog.com/blog/ cloudkick-presents-at-under-the-radar-2009*.

Index

About the Author

 **Richard Banks** is a principle interaction designer for Microsoft Research in Cambridge, UK. He's part of a team that spends most of its time looking at family life, trying to understand the complexities of home, in order to figure out how the digital should fit in appropriately. Richard joined Microsoft in 2005 after graduating from the Royal College of Art in London. Since then he's worked as a design manager in Seattle on Microsoft's Office, Windows, and MSN products before moving home and into Microsoft Research. Richard holds in excess of twenty patents for design work at Microsoft and is a Fellow of the Royal Society of Arts in the UK.

What do you think of this book?

We want to hear from you!
To participate in a brief online survey, please visit:

microsoft.com/learning/booksurvey

Tell us how well this book meets your needs—what works effectively, and what we can do better. Your feedback will help us continually improve our books and learning resources for you.

Thank you in advance for your input!